AMERICANS in DENMARK

Comparisons of the
Two Cultures by
Writers, Artists, and Teachers

Edited and with an Introduction by
F. Richard Thomas

Afterword by

Peter Vinten-Johansen

Southern Illinois University Press

Carbondale and Edwardsville

DL

142

A43

A44

1990

14 8669

may 1990

Library of Congress Cataloging-in-Publication Data

Americans in Denmark: comparisons of the two cultures by writers,
artists, and teachers/edited by F. Richard Thomas
    p. cm.
    Bibliography: p.
    1. Americans—Denmark—Attitudes. 2. Denmark—Civiliza-
tion—Public opinion. 3. United States—Civilization—Public
opinion. 4. Public opinion—Denmark. I. Thomas, F. Richard.
    DL142.A43A44   1990
    948.9'00413—dc19
    ISBN 0–8093–1536–X   88-38908
                                                              CIP

for Ameridanes, especially Sherry, Caeri, and Severn

Contents

Acknowledgments

Besides the contributors whose work appears here, many other Americans who live in Denmark sent material that did not fit the final format of the book. I extend my sincere appreciation to all of these people, especially the following: Emmanuel K. Abdul Rahim, Henrik Christiansen, Glen Frommer, Fradley Garner, Ralph Grant, Alice Cobb Ipsen, Sam Jackson, Shirley Madsen, Lauri Nissen, Sahib Shihab, Kathleen Tommerup.

Both friends and strangers who offered invaluable suggestions and/or assistance include Sidsil Brun, Bob Bryan, Carol A. Burns, Margot Gunzenhauser, Elsebeth Hurup, Johannes Ipsen, Stuart McIntyre, Gail Meltzer, Nathalie Melzer, Patricia Miles, Suzyn Moore, Janine Morgall, David Nye, Dan Seiters, Karen Kirk Sørensen, Grey Stephenson, Ed Thigpen, Sharon Thomas, and Rikk Towle.

Reed Baird, Orla Christensen, Thomas Kennedy, Ed Thomasson, and Peter Vinten-Johansen deserve special recognition for giving assistance far beyond what I expected.

I am sorry I cannot individually thank the scores of people with whom I had social, incidental, and telephone conversations on this book's topic, for all of this information has helped me write the introductory essay and plan my editorial strategy. I hope they will understand the omission of their names.

An earlier version of the introductory essay, "Americans in Denmark," appeared in *The Workshop* 25 (October 1987), a publication of the Engelsk Institut of Odense University, Denmark.

I thank also the Department of American Thought and Language at Michigan State University and, finally, the Engelsk Institut at Odense University, which supported and encouraged me while I collected essays during my tenure as a Fulbright Grantee in 1985–86.

I of course take responsibility for the shortcomings of the book.

AMERICANS in DENMARK

had actually lived three full years, nonconsecutively, in one place: Denmark.

Why did we keep coming back to Denmark? Why did we want to keep coming back? We had often told each other that we should live in Denmark for a longer period of time, perhaps permanently. Something about the country seemed to stimulate our creativity— my poetry, my wife's fiction, and the teaching and scholarship in which we're both involved. We also have secure jobs in the States. Given the prospect of moving to a new country with no jobs in hand, few possibilities for the future, and a Danish government that discourages foreign workers, we were never courageous enough to make the move. Nevertheless, I was interested in discovering what Americans in Denmark felt about their emigration from the United States to a new country. Perhaps one day our chance would come, too, and I wanted to know what to expect. Indeed, I wanted to know if undertaking a move of such magnitude involved courage or foolishness. Did the four thousand Americans who live in Denmark relish or regret their decision to leave the United States? More specifically, in light of our lifelong interests, did the writers, artists, and teachers who live in Denmark relish or regret their decision?

To find the answer to this question and discover the reasons for the answer, I drafted a series of questions (see chapter 2) and sent them over a two-year period to as many writers, artists, and teachers as I could find.

Having taught writing for over twenty years, I knew that I did not want to interview people. I had used interviewing strategies as prewriting exercises in my classes for many years, and it was clear to me that what students say to begin with is much different from what they write to end with. I knew this to be true as well in my own writing. In other words, the writing process is also a creative thinking process. If I could get Americans to write about their experiences in Denmark, I assumed I would receive, for the most part, reasonably tight, carefully deliberated (rather than spontaneous) responses. These could contain truly educational, enlightening insights, and if I could get people to write essays, not just answer questions, the responses would also reflect the writers' personalities: their individuality, their dreams, perhaps even their covert biases and prejudices. Therefore, I pleaded with those to whom I sent the list of questions: "These questions are only to get you to think about what living in Denmark has meant to you. I hope they will inspire you to write a two- to ten-page essay about your living in Denmark. If you don't have time to write an essay, you are welcome to write answers to the questions."

The results of my inquiry cannot be graphed or quantified with any accuracy. These essays do, however, reflect the integrity of individuals who reveal the complex process of the mind and body coming to terms with a new environment. And while the following essays and responses certainly do not represent the views of all Americans living in Denmark, they do offer clues to the issues, problems, joys, and challenges that not only writers, teachers, scholars, and artists, but all Americans who live abroad must confront. All emigrants are constantly faced with unasked questions. Is my new life developing here the way I want it to? Does my work suffer or become enriched in this new environment? Am I happy with this environment? Does this environment have anything to do with how happy I am with myself? In short, am I relishing or regretting my decision to live in Denmark? The first inclination of anyone faced with these questions is to try to compare the advantages and disadvantages of the two different cultures.

A Comparison of the Two Cultures. Although I cannot quantify or draw graphs, I can easily summarize the comparisons that are most often made between Denmark and the United States, not only from having lived in Denmark and having talked to a great number of Americans in Denmark, but especially from having read both the following essays and the many shorter answers to my questions. Although the next few pages are written as if all of the contributors unanimously agreed, such is definitely not the case, as the reader will see from the individual responses. Some observations, however, are repeated often enough to merit generalization. .

Overwhelmingly, Americans who live in Denmark look back on the United States as a land of improvisation, innovation, and opportunity. They either state explicitly or assume that there are no rituals or traditions of sufficient power ("History is bunk," says Henry Ford) to limit one's thinking and one's creative abilities in the United States. Because there are few constraining rituals, Americans seem to have a flexible, open, "let's-see-what-happens" attitude not found in Denmark, which as a one-thousand-year-old kingdom has developed an unwritten protocol for social, political, and intellectual behavior. For example, the inclination of Americans who grew up with few restrictive traditions is to solve problems, not just to talk about them: bomb Libya, send a person to the moon, create a new machine, back the Contras, develop a vaccine.

Correspondingly, Americans lacking the obvious restrictions of ritual and tradition are perceived to be more individualistic, more willing to try something new and to take a risk—in business, politics, or the arts—than their Danish counterparts. In this sense, Americans appear to some of the writers in this book to be more creative, and because they are individually involved in what they are doing, they appear to be more enthusiastic, optimistic, and excited about their efforts. Seeing results is not only possible, but expected.

Furthermore, in American society, where a prescribed national procedure for aiding the unfortunate has never been established, individual volunteer work is accepted, often expected, usually rewarded publicly, and appears to provide the volunteer with self-satisfaction.

Not only because of the emphasis on individualism—and loneliness that can accompany individualism—but because of social and geographic mobility and the separation from family, Americans in Denmark frequently consider themselves more open, friendly, and helpful to newcomers, whether to new neighbors or to visiting foreigners, than Danes have been towards them.

Because America is so large and contains so many different types of people, many contributors to this anthology also perceive the United States as a land of variety: in food, lifestyles, races, religions, landscapes, and so on. Patricia Johnson, a young black woman in Odense (where racial differences are rare) misses "the huge assortment of colors/cultures that we have in the United States." Furthermore, she says, "I get so tired of Danes staring at me, . . . [and] it's still annoying when children gesticulate at me or the more daring ones ask me where in Africa I come from." (This and the following brief quotations in this introduction are from the responses of Americans whose entire essays are not included.)

The size of the United States and its relatively few people per square mile, by European standards, has heightened the emigrants' impression of it as an intact, wild, unplanned, and natural landscape—an impression that encourages them to contrast the seemingly raw, organic, natural, chaotic, energetic mentality in the United States with what they see as a more restricted, formal, and artificial European landscape and mentality.

The other side of the coin is the emigrants' perception that the American workshop of individualism may destroy as many people as it encourages and supports. Many Americans in Denmark acknowledge that the current American Dream—that anyone can achieve economic and social success if he or she is just willing to try—is an unrealizable dream for most people. Many who try to make it to the top meet with obstacles for which they are not prepared: discrimination, yes, but also the realization that their principles will not allow them to engage in the competition and exploitation of the free enterprise capitalist system. The American system seems to encourage the worship of commercialism rather than high standards of excellence, a cultural weakness that many American emigrants find less prevalent in Denmark. The infiltration of American commercial values into politics—for example, television used to "sell" a President or to "sell" Star Wars—is also considered deplorable by some Americans living in Denmark. "What I didn't like about the United States," says librarian Philip Glaser, "[was] the advertising, the twenty-four-hour-a-day selling mentality that permeates the place."

The contributors often criticized the American political system because it does not allow the representation of minority ideologies in Congress. Compared with Denmark, where thirteen parties battle out their differences in Parliament—giving a greater number of minority viewpoints official voice in government—the United States has only two barely distinquishable parties. The American system, the emigrants feel, thereby disallows minority ideas and opinions, ensures that minority protest will be strident, guarantees that many

of the disenfranchised will not vote, and encourages civil disobe-
dience.

Many contributors also view America as a sexual quagmire. It
is perhaps the only industrialized country in the Western world that
attempts to legislate sexual morality. Witness, for example, the state
laws that prohibit sexual practices among consenting adults, even
in the privacy of their homes. Sex in the United States is not only
considered naughty, perhaps even lewd in itself, but it is frequently
associated with violence—usually against women. A relentless bar-
age of exploitative, manipulative, and often demeaning sexual activity pervades the American media. Yet healthy, natural, nonviolent
sexual activity is taboo—it is rarely shown on television, encouraged
between the sexes, or even discussed in schools with boys and girls
together. For many Americans who live in Denmark, the fear of the
open expression of natural sexuality in the United States encourages
inequalities between the sexes, teenage pregnancies (the United
States has the highest per capita rate of all the industrialized nations),
and violent sex crimes. American women in Denmark would think
twice before returning to the States, where many of them feel that
being anywhere alone, especially after dark, exposes them to the
constant threat of violence.

Several other concerns are expressed by Americans in Denmark.
Some deplore the individual American's lack of political awareness.
They also lament that the United States is a world power that med-
dles unilaterally in the affairs of other countries. They believe America's cowboy mentality, or rugged individualism, while it can be
admirable, encourages too little thought before action—especially in
the political arena.

The contributors also appear tired of the constant, fast-paced,
sometimes hysterical activity in the United States and feel an injec-
tion of European-style calm and reflection would be therapeutic. For
example, glassworker Pete Hunner feels that "one real difference
between Denmark and the United States is the pace of life. In the
States if you're on the bandwagon and you want to take a pause and
get off for awhile, by the time you want to get back on again, the
bandwagon's gone too far for you to catch up with it. In Copenhagen,
everything is at a much slower, more realistic pace. You can get off,

catch up, and get back on. Where I live, on the Danish island of Bornholm, the bandwagon stops and waits for you if you want to take a break."

In summation, on the negative side, many Americans in Denmark consider the United States a land of crime, violence, and insecurity, lacking peace and safety. It does not appear to them to be a place where women, children, or the elderly (especially if they are poor, unemployed, or of the "wrong" color) would choose to live if they experienced and became attached to another, less risky, way of life—if, for example, they had lived in Denmark.

But Americans in Denmark are not starry-eyed about their adoptive country; many of them are very critical of Denmark, too. They frequently complain about the Danish language. As Lisa Nagle writes, Danish "is impossible for me to pronounce and was more difficult to learn than German, French, Spanish, and Kiswahili put together." The following are also common subjects of complaint: the weather (which can be cold, gray, and rainy the year round), the television programming (the lack of variety on Denmark's one channel), the reserve and lack of openness of many Danes, and the lack of variety in the food. Finally, as Caroline Olson observes, "*Den Dejlige Lille Land* (the nice little country) is an overworked epithet, and the nationalism it reflects can grate."

By far the most common criticism by Americans who have immigrated to Denmark is directed toward what they perceive as a Danish penchant to worship the group at the expense of the individual. To them, Danish protocol and traditions often lead to a peculiar form of Danish conservatism that supports lengthy discussion (about political, social, and educational environments, for example) and few, often very slow, behavioral changes. In fact, spontaneity and its accompanying enthusiasm are often grounds for suspicion and ostracism. At birthday parties and Christmas celebrations or at lunch in the canteen, conformity to tradition is a virtual requirement. Guests will walk around the block several times in order not to arrive at a host's home early. When they do arrive, they can expect a dinner very much like every other dinner they have ever attended, from the welcoming drink to the final coffee. As musician Mark Kline says, "Danish predictability can be reassuring and enjoyable, certainly, but as a Kansan, I prefer a more let's-see-what-happens attitude."

In education, teaching to the group means teaching to the middle and can, according to these American emigrants, encourage mediocrity in the public schools. Bright students are bored and often attend private schools. Furthermore, Danes are so democratic and children so respected that students seem to have rights far beyond what students would have in the States. Whereas most teachers in the States would find the extension of democracy to the classroom very difficult, some teachers in Denmark have consciously attempted to instill it. An obvious outcome is the presence of students who think they have the right to be disruptive if they wish. In other words, children in Denmark are not treated like children in the United States, where the word *child* usually implies one who is not yet capable of making sound judgments.

Danes apparently look upon volunteer work with some disdain because it not only takes jobs away from workers in the group but is also demeaning. Furthermore, the poor and criminals, for example, are not really responsible for their condition—they are the way they are because of the failing of the group to deal with the causes of their problems. As a result, Danes are less inclined to feel individually responsible for their own shortcomings, whereas Americans usually do blame the individual for his or her shortcomings.

Many Americans in Denmark also decry what they consider excessive legal controls on the movement of individuals. Everyone is registered with the government and must carry a registration card. Changes of address are required within five days of moving. Taxes can be taken directly from personal bank accounts. The government can borrow from an individual's savings in a personal bank account. Police issue speeding tickets without stopping drivers: the owner of a car receives a ticket in the mail with a picture of the car, upon which is printed the excessive speed and the amount of the fine. "Big Brother's decisions," says Caroline Olson, "intrude more on my life here [than in the States]; do I really want the government to decide that I must have five weeks of vacation, some at specified times of the year, and mandate forced withholding each month in a vacation account?" In many cases, the group's desire for order and stability prevails over the individual's desire for spontaneity and freedom of action.

Mentioned several times in the following contributions is a codification of group mentality called *Janteloven* (the "Law of Jante"). In 1933 Aksel Sandemose—a Dane who was himself an immigrant in Norway from the time he was thirty years old—coined the term in a novel entitled *A Fugitive Crosses His Tracks* (trans. Eugene Gay-Tifft, New York: Knopf, 1936). Espen Arnakke, the Danish protaganist and first-person narrator of the novel, commits a murder when he is but a young man. As we learn, the conformist values of Espen's hometown of Jante—values that destroyed the individualistic spirit of his boyhood—are directly responsible for the murder. The culpable "Law of Jante" has ten commandments:

1. Thou shalt not believe thou art something.
2. Thou shalt not believe thou art as good as we.
3. Thou shalt not believe thou art more wise than we.
4. Thou shalt not fancy thyself better than we.
5. Thou shalt not believe thou knowest more than we.
6. Thou shalt not believe thou art greater than we.
7. Thou shalt not believe thou amountest to anything.
8. Thou shalt not laugh at us.
9. Thou shalt not believe that anyone is concerned with thee.
10. Thou shalt not believe thou canst teach us anything.

(77–78)

Although Sandemose himself did not insist that these laws were exclusively Danish (Espen Arnakke encountered them everywhere in his travels), they have at least come to be associated with Nordic values, perhaps only because Sandemose is a Danish-Norwegian author.

Most Danes and Americans in Denmark I have met are familiar with the "Law of Jante," and are aware that it is a satirical attack on provincialism and the coincidental jealousy of those who achieve beyond the proscriptions of their narrow community. Many Danes and most Americans in Denmark I have met also believe that the "Law of Jante," which epitomizes the negative values of a group mentality (as opposed to an individualistic mentality), is more applicable to Danish society than to American society. Writer Ed Kowalski, a respondent to my questionnaire who is frequently positive about many Danish values, believes Sandemose's literary metaphor characterizes the Danish work ethic and sharply distinguishes it from that of the United States: "In America a person works hard and is successful; other Americans look at him or her and say, 'If he can do it, so can I,' and work hard at achieving that goal. If a Dane works hard and achieves success, other Danes look at him or her and say, 'Look at that creep—it's disgusting—let's do what we can to tear him or her down to our lower level.' " Kowalski's condemnation may be harsh, but it is not unique. In fact, I have heard Danes refer to the the "Law of Jante" (sometimes in jest, but also seriously) if they, themselves, or fellow Danes appear to transcend the boundaries established by the group.

Without having read Sandemose's book, most American emigrants in Denmark who have heard of the "Law of Jante" understand it to be a metaphor for a group mentality that discourages individualism and individual achievement, novelty of thought and action, spontaneity, variety, and competition, while encouraging sameness, insidious deceitfulness, jealousy, mediocrity, and complacency, traits that these Americans find more characteristically Danish than American.

Of course Americans in Denmark also have positive comments about Denmark. First of all, although the group mentality can be oppressive, it can also be liberating when it connotes a sense of cooperation and caring for others in a way that seems lacking on a national level in the United States. Indeed, as opposed to the cutthroat, survival-of-the-fittest assumptions that the emigrants tend to believe underlie American society, they view Danes as feeling that everyone has a right to be taken care of by the group. Danes seem to believe that no one should have to ask for help from other individuals, for the government should take care of its citizens. The result is a liberating degree of personal security unrealized by most Americans who live in the United States.

Danish social democracy and the services that it supports seem to many emigrants to provide a sense of social equality among Danish citizens that is not found in the States. Communication between farmers, workers, citydwellers, laborers, and intellectuals is not uncommon. In Denmark (partly because of an apprenticeship system that encourages the notion that work well done serves not only the individual but also the common good) blue collar workers have pride in their jobs. For the most part, they do not seem to feel exploited or inferior. And if they do feel exploited, either their unions or one of the thirteen parties will often represent their views. Consequently, most Danes are politically aware and likely to vote in elections.

While the emigrants perceive little extreme wealth in Denmark, they also notice very little poverty. Because economic and medical security is guaranteed, which is perhaps partially responsible for the lower rate of violent crimes than in the United States, emigrants view their lives in Denmark as safe, secure, and stable.

Such security appears to encourage a remarkable degree of personal freedom in changing careers. Because a change in careers does not jeopardize medical insurance, retirement plans, or children's educational opportunities, one's lifelong career options are more varied than in the United States. The opportunities to become reeducated in a new career are many and inexpensive. Lifelong education is considered to be a necessity for Denmark's democratic society. It is not unusual, therefore, to find pensioners learning another language (perhaps their fourth or fifth) or a retirement vocation or avocation. The responsibility for this enlightened and peculiarly Danish view of education can be traced to the outstanding Christian philosopher, poet, politician, translator, and hymn writer N. F. S. Grundtvig (1783–1872) who inspired the world-renowned Danish folk high schools—schools that were established in the nineteenth century for the Danish citizenry to ensure their educated participation in a democratic society.

Danish children also appear to have more world knowledge than American children, perhaps because they live in a small country in Europe and the intensive study of at least two other languages besides Danish is a significant part of their education. Because of the emphasis on lifelong education and because insurance and retirement benefits are nationalized, Danish students do not seem to be pushed, as American students are, to hurry and finish their education or to find a job in order to buy into the health and retirement benefits of their prospective employers.

Americans in Denmark generally find sexuality in Denmark altogether wholesome and relaxed as compared to that in the United States. Men do not need to be macho. Women do not need to be flirts. But men can easily be masculine, and women can be feminine. Casual sexual relationships do not destroy reputations, nor do non-sexual relationships. Public nudity is not just accepted; one would be surprised to hear someone object to it. Sex education programs are shown on public television for children, as are nudity and expressions of sexuality. Sexual attraction between men and women has apparently not suffered, and the incidence of sex crimes is much lower in Denmark than in the United States.

In summary, a great number of Americans in Denmark suggest that Denmark, with its low level of poverty and crime, its ability to provide more than basic necessities for most of its citizens, and its superior educational opportunities deserves its very high ranking—much higher than that of the United States—on any international surveys on the quality of life. For a great number of the American emigrants, Denmark is a suitably democratic, egalitarian, peaceful, calm, safe, secure, stable, and very clean place to live. "When I think about one day settling down with a family," writes Mark Wheat, "I often think of Denmark. It's reassuring to think whatever happens to me, my children would be given the best of care in a land relatively safe and remarkably civilized by global standards." It is perhaps also an ideal place for the elderly.

On Creativity.   Although the emigrants' observations about the United States and Denmark would help inform any decision I might make about whether to immigrate to Denmark, they did not help me as much as I had hoped to understand why my own, short-term, serial experiences living in Denmark seemed to sharpen my creativity. In fact, responses to my question, "Do you think your creativity is enhanced by living in Denmark?," varied considerably.

The presence, over several decades, of a large number of excellent jazz musicians in Copenhagen—most of them black—suggests a favorable climate for their creativity. Ben Webster, Kenny Drew, Thad Jones, Dexter Gordon, Stuff Smith, Ed Thigpen, Ernie Wilkins, Duke Jordan, Doug Rainey, and Mercer Ellington (who recently donated a large collection of his father's tapes to Denmark's national broadcasting system) are but a few of the musicians who either now live or have lived in Denmark.

On the other hand, Ed Kowalski expresses an opinion that reflects the worst of the *Janteloven* group mentality. It is an opinion that I have heard from a number of foreigners, not just Americans, as well as Danes. "What about creativity? Completely suffocated in Denmark. The arts are controlled by cliques. If you don't think and act the same, you are excluded. I have submitted television and film manuscripts that aren't even looked at because, 'I have the wrong attitude.' (I wrote often for television in the States.) 'Where are your papers from an authorized school that show you are talented?' If you write or draw what the group in power wants to hear, you have a chance of success. If you write something critical or out-of-line, you had better try another profession."

But other emigrants express contrasting viewpoints. For example, Pete Hunner says, "I definitely think my creativity is enhanced by living in Denmark. . . . My glass work is inspired by the changes in the fields and the light and the color in the water and the heavens."

Dancer/choreographer Warren Spears, who danced with Alvin Ailey, feels that his creativity is enhanced because "in Denmark I have no fear of failure and not being able to create again." He feels this in part because Danes appear to be more open to experimental works than Americans. The Danes "give artists a chance, not judging them at every performance, but taking into account the artist as a whole . . . the bulk of his or her work. . . . [As a result] I have grown as an artist and as a person. . . . If and when I go back to the States, I'll return with the product of my stay here in Denmark—the openness and the free chance to develop."

The key to the reason why Denmark seemed to enhance both my wife's and my creativity and productivity does not lie exclusively in what the particular environment itself has to offer, but more in what we discovered about ourselves by living in a different environment that is sometimes strange and uncomfortable despite its many positive qualities. Musician Mark Kline speaks for many artists in his observation that "for me the 'identity crisis' [of moving to a different culture] has not been a crisis at all, but a positive growth of self-awareness. I needed to experience a different way of life, a different outlook on what goes on in our world. I saw and am seeing things I like and don't like here. I learned and am learning to accept differences. After living here for some time, I began to understand better who I am and why I am who I am. The key has been the contrasts. Maybe it is something similar to the thought that we understand sunlight because there is darkness. Now I know much better who I am, and I've made an interesting discovery: I'm much less an American than a Kansan, and less a Kansan than a Chase Countian. There is so much about me that is a consequence of having lived twenty-eight years on a farm in Chase County. Many of my values and memories, my humor and my relatively easygoing manner—these and much more—are things that I never thought so much about before. But now there are times when I feel I stand in screaming contrast to the rest of Copenhagen—and I don't mind it. I enjoy being different."

To "enjoy being different" is probably something that all American emigrants in Denmark have to learn if they are to become creative and productive. Most of them have discovered that while they may adapt to Denmark, they will never really consider themselves Danes.

In fact, a recurring theme in many of the following essays is the idea that being in the middle, some place between Denmark and the United States—limbo, perhaps—may be a condition that is especially conducive to creativity (see chapter 4).

American emigrants may love Denmark and the United States at the same time, and at the same time hate aspects of both countries. Their lives are in Denmark but they know that they will never be Danes. Nevertheless, having lived in Denmark and established family and friends, they wonder if they can truly go home again—in mind and spirit as well as in body. Most of them probably cannot, because they have chosen, perhaps unwittingly, to become true citizens of the world by being neither Danish nor American. This is not only a source of identity for them, but a source of anxiety as well. It is their boon and their bane. Like first generation immigrants anywhere, they belong to neither country entirely and find themselves living in limbo. On the other hand, such a state of limbo can contribute markedly to their creativity and productivity.

This discussion of limbo and its relationship to creativity leads naturally to a discussion of other immigrant studies. While no one, as far as I know, has ever looked at Americans in Denmark, many studies have dealt with immigration to the United States, including the large number of Scandinavian immigrants. A few studies have examined Danes in America, and several have looked at Americans in other parts of the world, especially non-Scandinavian Europe. What is clear from all of these studies is that limbo—however it is called—is a universal immigrant experience.

Oscar Handlin's *The Uprooted* (1951), is the seminal book in the field of immigrant studies that reveals, as does this study, the problems of immigration from "the perspective of the individual received rather than of the receiving society" (4). Handlin's study of the nineteenth century shows that "the history of immigration is a history of alienation and its consequences" (4). For the immigrants "without the whole complex of institutions and social patterns which formerly guided their actions . . . every act was crucial, the product of conscious weighing of alternatives, never simple conformity to an habitual pattern. No man could escape choices that involved, day after day, an evaluation of his goals, of the meaning of his existence, and of the purpose of the social forms and institutions that surrounded him" (6). The immigrants ultimately learned that they lived "under the shadow of a consciousness that they would never belong. They had thus completed their alienation from the culture to which they had come, as from that which they had left" (285). In short, they were in limbo.

More specifically related to Scandinavia is *The Divided Heart: Scandinavian Immigrant Experience through Literary Sources* (1974) by Dorothy Burton Skårdal (who originally wrote this book as a dissertation under Oscar Handlin). It is perhaps the most comprehensive of the studies that reveal the conseqeuences of limbo and alienation, the ways in which Scandinavian immigrants in America were divided betweeen the Old World and the New. "When a person leaves the culture in which his personality was formed," writes Skårdal, and plunges into a society whose ways are strange to him but where he means to stay, the confrontation will force him into painful personal change. This cultural shock was common and central to all immigrant experience" (20).

As for Danish immigrants to the United States, two recent books, George R. Nielsen's *The Danish Americans* (1981) and Frederick Hale's *Danes in North America* (1984), show the rapid assimilation of many Danes (most of whom immigrated before 1914) into American society. But they also show that a great many of these Danes claimed loyalty to both countries and resisted total assimilation by forming societies and organizations that helped them preserve their Danish heritage. And Hale's book, a collection of letters written by Danish immigrants, reveals that many Danes were unable to withstand the pressures of being an immigrant and returned home to Denmark.

But these are books about immigrants to America. What about studies of emigrants from America? Of the books written about Americans abroad (see the Selected Bibliography for several), few of them deal in any detailed way with the personal problems of emigration, perhaps because few of them deal with Americans who seriously intend to stay in their adoptive country. Nevertheless, Ernest Earnest's *Expatriates and Patriots: American Artists, Scholars, and Writers in Europe* (1968) does suggest a limbo phenomenon: "The evidence derived from this examination of the lives and work of representative artists, scholars, and writers from the time of Irving to 1929 leads to the conclusion that the artist and intellectual has not been rejected by his own country nor has he as a rule become a spiritual expatriate" (280). John Bainbridge in *Another Way of Living: A Gallery of Americans Who Chose to Live in Europe* (1968) coined the term *Ameropeans* to describe those contemporary Americans who choose to live in Europe but expect to return to the United States. He clearly shows Ameropeans caught between two cultures:

"Their heart is in America. Their home is in Europe. They embrace both. They have become a part of both, and they will remain a part of both, whether or not they ever go home to live" (7). Furthermore, his interviewees compare living in the United States and living in Europe, and they sometimes comment about the influence of their foreign environment on their creativity. Aside from the fact that Bainbridge uses interviews instead of written essays, that he interviews no Danes or Scandinavians ("I found very few Ameropeans in Scandinavia" [11]), and that he does not focus on American artists, writers, and teachers in Europe, his study does have similarities to my own.

My own study of Americans in Denmark, however, does not deal with Americans who expect to return to the United States. In fact, most of the contributors to this volume cannot expect to return to the States permanently if they are to maintain relationships with their Danish families and friends. Yet most of these Americans also realize that they are but five hours away from the United States— at least for a visit. In other words, the contemporary immigrant experience is necessarily much different (unless the immigrant is in exile) from the immigrant experience of the nineteenth century that required a long and arduous trip via sea in which shipboard death was not unusual. Nevertheless, it is clear from the essays in this book as well as from the other studies mentioned that limbo is a given for the immigrant, regardless of the degree of finality of the physical break with the mother country.

The fact that limbo also provides impetus for creativity has been discovered by others besides myself. For example, Jane Katz in her book *Artists in Exile* (1983), after studying twenty-four artists (poets, writers, dancers, painters, and so forth) who emigrated from their restrictive home societies to the United States, writes: "The uprooted artist's ties with the past are torn, but not severed—one's ethnic identity is a source of strength. In his creative work, the artist links past and present, perceiving meaning in both" (xxiii). "Danger and insecurity," says Handlin in *The Uprooted*, "are other words for freedom and opportunity" (304). As Franklin D. Scott says in his collection of essays entitled *World Migration in Modern Times* (1968): "Constant confrontation with new situations in nature and in social relationships demands adaptation and creativity, [and] leads to invention and development. . . . Creativity or invention is most vigorous where the challenge of the new situation is strongest (if not too strong)" (1, 5). As it is in Denmark, one might add.

A correlative source of creativity and productivity (and one which would be different for the modern Dane or European immigrating to the United States) manifests itself in reading the answers to the questions I asked and in talking to these Americans. Americans in Denmark feel that they are living in the world. In Denmark one can feel one's immediate connection, not only to Scandinavia, but to the rest of Europe and to the United States as well. Perhaps because America is so large and powerful, or perhaps because of its ideal of a uni-cultural, self-centered educational system, most people in the United States don't feel connected to the wider world outside the United States. Americans who live in Denmark feel that they would relinquish that sense of interdependence with the rest of the world by returning to the United States.

Because by living abroad they have learned about the interdependence of the peoples and nations of the world and because their unique condition forces them to stand outside of any culture, some of the authors in this book have already made significant contributions toward international communication and understanding. And almost all of the authors in this book have relinquished most of the nationalistic chauvinism they may have had. While the emotional safisfactions of provincialism may be lessened as a result, their creative work in all areas—not only in teaching, writing, and the arts—is enriched.

My own creativity has definitely been enriched by living in Denmark because there I feel connected to the rest of the world and stimulated by a variety of cultural values. I have become a creature in cultural limbo, someone who is drawn to Denmark and to the United States, standing apart from both—someone who now views himself and his world with very different eyes after living in Denmark. This new and exciting perspective—a cosmopolitan, multicultural consciousness resulting from my life in limbo between the United States and Denmark—does at times cause me considerable anxiety, but it always enhances my creativity.

American expatriate artists and writers of the nineteenth century, the 1920s, and even today, frequently extol European beauty, tradition, and high regard for the sensual pleasures. While these qualities are certainly inspirational, the emigrants' feeling of living both in limbo and in the world may be equally responsible for their enhanced creativity.

Conclusions.   Our family remains unresolved about permanently moving to Denmark. To make such a move a certain amount of happenstance seems necessary for most people. For example, most of the contributors to this book are in Denmark because at one point in their lives, either while traveling in Europe or perhaps while going to school in the United States, they fell in love with a Dane. Indeed, some Americans are in Denmark because of their personal reactions to the Vietnam War or to racism in the United States (a former Congress of Racial Equality member decided not to submit his reactions) or because of the excellent jazz environment, especially for black musicians. But they are the exception. Few Americans in this anthology decided to move to Denmark because they were unable to tolerate their living conditions in the United States, because they were at odds with the political climate, or because they believed that their creativity would be enhanced.

If our family decides to move to Denmark, it will be for the following reasons. We have learned to accept our having been nurtured for fifty years in the competitive, individualistic school of the American Dream, which taught us (sometimes for better and sometimes for worse) that individual goals are possible and worth striving for, and we have learned that individualism and the goals of a group-oriented culture are not necessarily mutually exclusive. We have learned to appreciate living in a group-oriented country that cares for and attempts to extend a viable quality to the lives of all of its citizens. We have learned to appreciate and use creatively the ambivalent feelings associated with living in limbo between the United States and Denmark. And, finally, we have learned to appreciate living in the world.

If we decide not to move to Denmark, it will be because we

have found that traveling back and forth in this mobile age of cheap air fares offers our family the opportunity to have the best of both worlds: the financial security of our established careers in the United States and the intermittent creative enrichment that comes from living abroad.

Our reasons for wanting to live in Denmark—to feel the excitement of being creative world citizens in a hospitable environment—may be similar to those of many of the early expatriate writers and artists whom I once regarded with esteem for romantic rather than realistic reasons. I discovered that some of the contributors to this anthology did not want to be considered expatriates—a term loaded with anti-American connotations. Though the term does not have these negative connotations to me, I can understand their concern. In many ways, the contributors to this book, while perhaps not patriots in the strictest sense, are not necessarily unpatriotic either. We need a new word for those who have an international perspective and are patriotic to an international community, as many of the people in this book are. Perhaps, for those who live in Europe, and even those who expect to stay in Europe, John Bainbridge's term Ameropeans is appropriate.

I have organized the following essays and other responses to my questionnaire under chapter headings that illustrate the issues raised in this introduction: "Comparing the Two Cultures: Denmark and the United States," "Limbo," "Living in the World," and "A New Home in Denmark." Individual contributors often deal with several, sometimes all, of these topics. I have not included a special chapter for creativity because this issue is integral, either explicitly or implicitly, to all of the essays. The chapters entitled "Limbo" and "Living in the World," however, are especially germane to the topic of creativity. The chapter immediately following this introduction, "Answering the Questions," acquaints the reader with the initial questionnaire provided to all of the contributors. A chapter of "Impressions" includes excerpts from essays that I was unable to use in their entirety. The afterword interprets the contributors' perceptions of cultural harmony and misalliance in general.

2

Answering the Questions

Every potential contributor was sent a list of questions. The following two contributors responded simply by answering the questions, which I include in this form so the reader can see how these established a framework for the kind of information I received. These respondents are respected artists in Copenhagen. Valjean is an institution himself, very well known for his multimedia theatrical productions; Thomas E. Kennedy is a well-known writer in the American community in Denmark.

Paul Valjean

Why do you live in Denmark?

Work.

Why do you not live in the United States?

There's more need for me here.

What do you miss about the United States?

Energy, engagement, action.

What do you think (or know) you would miss about Denmark if you returned to the United States to live?

Danish gentleness and *hygge* (cozy, homelike comfort).

Have you ever thought about returning to the United States to live?

Yes, to check out the cultural situation.

What do you find wrong with Denmark, even though you live here?

The psychological and intellectual restrictions imposed by the *"Jante"* law (see chapter 1).

What would you like to change about the United States?

Hyprocrisy as a way of life.

What do you feel is good about the United States?

The belief that life is worth living.

What do you think is good about Denmark?

The belief that life is worth living primarily with others.

Can you make any comparisons between Denmark and the United States about the quality of your life?

In Denmark a lifestyle can be maintained independent of income and still be socially acceptable.

If you are involved in arts, crafts, teaching, performing, scholarship, or some related field, do you think your creativity is enhanced by living in Denmark?

No, creativity and inspiration are imported.

Do you think you make any contributions (artistic, political, social, personal, etc.) to Danish society and/or culture? American society and/or culture? Do you attach any importance to this?

Yes, at least the Danes think so, which is the prime reason for my residence in Denmark. There is little evidence that this reflects upon my American citizenship. Because I'm an artist, my thinking is more universal than national.

Thomas E. Kennedy

Why do you live in Denmark? Why do you not live in the United States?

I decided that I wished to live in Denmark during a visit in 1972 when I lost my way late at night and found myself wandering through narrow, dark, echoing, cobblestoned streets in a state of complete relaxation. It occurred to me that had I lost my way in New York, my hometown, late at night in, say, Central Park (which I did, in fact, once do), I would have been walking in fear and trembling. The fear level in New York is, of course, partially subjective. However, when I lived on the lower east side, I was given to learn fear through a number of object lessons. The most vivid lesson of all consisted of seven M-1 bullet holes in the metal door of my Norwegian girlfriend's apartment on East Second Street, just around the corner from me. Her neighbor did it, enraged that her faucet kept dripping. It took me about two years to fully relax after leaving the States for Europe. I lived in the French countryside for the first year and was bored, but got a lot of writing done (wasn't much else to do). I moved to Denmark in 1976, having engineered a consultancy that would support me, and it took a couple of years to tune into Danish ways. Since then, I have felt quite calm. I like feeling that way. I feel like myself at last.

What do you miss about the United States?

Baseball; Frank Sinatra; Chinese laundries; Fifth Avenue; the Oak Bar at the Plaza; the teeming streets; the deserts of the Southwest; the Atlantic shelf (which makes for tub-warm swimming water in July); the sweaty, hot summers; fried breakfasts (Danes retch at the aroma of frying bacon or sausage in the morning); all those wonderful bookstores (remainders!); big cheap drinks in bars (the Danes measure out their gin most meanly—it's controlled by law); great fat steaks for a relative pittance; built-in closets; the language (the slang, jive, rhythms of the street-talkin' dudes); the undemanding tolerance of varied behavior that one finds in the best parts of the melting pot; the optimism (the feeling that whatever it is you set out to do you can get it done one way or another, that you're not going to walk nose first into an impenetrable wall of bureaucracy); the sweet-eyed warmth of American women; the blaring rock issuing from just about everywhere; all those great restaurants and bars; all those beaches; and cheap goods (relatively)—cars, furniture, clothes—all of which makes for a great deal of convenience, but also a lot of garbage. I also miss the friendship patterns of men. Men do not seem to form friendships here to the extent that they do in the States. I know lots of Danes and I have a few Danish friends, yet I cannot enjoy my Danish male friends in the way that I can enjoy my American friends. This may have something to do with the fact that Danes in general are so very subtle—too subtle perhaps to tolerate the loud happy camaraderie that American men are famous for. All in all, though, what I miss most is the American language—a medium of understanding that puts you in a club of over 200 million people.

What do you think (or know) you would miss about Denmark if you returned to the United States to live?

What I would miss about Denmark is less tangible, I suppose, less readily identifiable—it's a cliché called the quality of life. If you fall down on the street, someone will probably stop to help you. More likely, half a dozen hands will shoot out to catch you. If you smile at someone, he or she will most likely smile back because you will be recognized as a human being rather than as a potential mass murderer. The general surroundings are calm, comfortable, and elegant. Danes live by the eye: color, design, and the arrangement of space are of vital interest to the everyday life of the Dane. Even in the state offices, the furnishings of civil service clerks are elegant and well appointed. Danes have a sense of responsibility and of shame, which might sometimes seem nerdy to the American spirit of individualism. If you put your feet up on the seat on the train, more than likely someone will scowl at you and ask you to take them down so as not to dirty the seat. Consequently, the Danish commuter train system is incredibly clean and well kept. All of Denmark is quite clean and calm, sometimes perhaps too calm, but not to worry: urbanism is on the way. The Hell's Angels held their world convention in Denmark last year, and it was well attended by local bikers.

Have you ever thought about returning to the United States to live?

Not really, not seriously, not yet anyway, although I would not exclude the occurrence of such a consideration in the not-too-distant future. The thing that keeps me from really considering it seriously just now is that my kids (six and four years old) will, I think, have a calmer, happier childhood here; of course, that is a hard, snobby judgment to make. I guess what I really mean is that I know they have it reasonably good here now, and I am not willing to take the chance of them not having it good in the States, because in the States, when you don't have it good, you have it, in my experience, god-awful.

What do you find wrong with Denmark, even though you live here?

The taxes are too high. You pay between 40 and 80 percent income tax as well as 22 percent blanket sales tax on everything, with higher rates on luxuries, like cigarettes, booze, and automobiles. Of course, you also have an extensive social coverage—more important, everybody has an extensive social coverage: free medical care, and that means everything; comprehensive free dental care for all children up to their teen years (which largely eliminates the need for extensive dental work for adults); free education from grade school through university, including medical school, and so on; excellent facilities for the care of the elderly (very humane conditions in this respect); well-kept roads; and fairly good welfare and pension coverage (though these still leave something to be desired). Therefore, what is wrong with Denmark is also what is right with it: high taxes but good social services. About the only things that bother me about Denmark are the tendency toward bourgeois hang-ups (but they are not inevitable—you can choose your own friends) and the tendency toward red tape and authoritarianism (though this is by no means as oppressive as it is in Sweden, for example). On balance, I find little to complain about here except for the weather, which really is miserable, although one can develop a taste for all sorts of spice, can't one?

What would you like to change about the United States?

If the United States could manage to strike a better balance between individual freedom and individual responsibility, between individual initiatives and responsible social programs, between social opportunity and social predestination, I think it would truly be the closest thing to paradise available on earth. The States has so much to offer, yet how can Americans love themselves when we allow people to die in the streets, to walk around in icy winters with their feet wrapped in rags? You can find any of a dozen corners in any of a dozen big American cities (and, no doubt, in rural areas of all fifty states as well) where you feel like you are gazing into the century before—such is the wretchedness that meets the eye. How can the nation tolerate this? Do we really believe that free will leads people to dereliction? Surely it is social predestination that is responsible for this.

CONTRIBUTORS

Paul Valjean was born in Michigan in 1935. He graduated from the Eastman School of Music and has worked since 1966 as a choreographer, director, composer, actor, consultant, and teacher in Copenhagen, where he is well known for his multimedia theatrical productions.

Thomas E. Kennedy has a B.A. from Fordham University and an M.F.A. in writing from Vermont College. He is the managing editor of the *Danish Medical Bulletin* and a writer of fiction. He lives in Hellerup near Copenhagen.

3

Comparing the Two Cultures: Denmark and the United States

While all of the authors in this anthology com-
pare Denmark and the United States, the fol-
lowing five essays are devoted to explicit cul-
tural comparisons. Sex, taxes, politics, religion,
freedom, welfare, security, spontaneity, vio-
lence, competition, quality of life, children, the
elderly, individuality, and creativity are recur-
ring issues compared in these responses.

THE FIRST STRAW

Ellen Bick Meier

> I'd rather live in Venice or Kyoto,
> except for the languages, but

> O really I don't care where I live or have lived.
> Wherever I am, young Sir, my wits about me,
>
> memory blazing, I'll cope & make do.
>
> John Berryman, "Roots"

It started with a straw. Although it is impossible to pinpoint the moments, gestures, and deeds that lead to the crucial decisions in our lives, my time in Denmark—eighteen years of it—springs from my habit of drinking soda with a straw.

Let me elaborate on this incredible assertion. Passing through Copenhagen in July 1967 on my way to Rome, I played truant one day from being a tourist. Instead, I found a local outdoor swimming pool and a deck chair on which to sunbathe and relax. Later, in line to buy a Coke, I asked the person in back of me what the Danish word for "straw" was. That person, two years later, was my husband.

Thus, I confess, I moved to Denmark not for career considerations or to study Isak Dinesen or Kirkegaard in the original, but because of a Dane. I'm not the only sinner either: many 1960s foreigners were wooed and won over by tall, blond, blue-eyed natives.

That confession does not explain, however, why I remained, as my Dane has since become my ex-husband. What could make a sun worshipper like me stick it out in a country with winters eight months long and income tax levels that start at 50 percent and move upward? Why? Am I a masochist? No, I stayed because of greed. By greed, I mean all the attention I received. When I made the move to Denmark in August 1968—I hit Danish shores just as waves from the Czech invasion hit—I was treated like a combination of Rockefeller, Margaret Mead, and Marilyn Monroe—if that combination doesn't sound totally unlikely. There were few foreigners then—people would compliment me on my brown eyes—and there were even fewer Americans. There were more than enough jobs for the ambitious and the talented. Jobs appeared in strange spots, like crocuses in midwinter. By 1970, I had my own radio talk show, I edited an English magazine on Scandinavia, and I could create my own courses at the university's English department. I was coaxed, cajoled, and spoiled rotten.

Despite some disdain for us because of Vietnam and United Fruit, we Americans were brown-eyed idols. Ben Webster and Dexter Gordon made the Copenhagen jazz club Montmartre internationally famous; multimedia artist Paul Valjean inspired and directed street theater and happenings throughout the 1970s; and Bob Dylan's guitarist Billy Cross settled in Copenhagen to perform, to produce records, and to marry a Dane.

But the times they are a-changin'. Brown eyes are no longer so unusual. During the 1970s, Denmark coaxed men from Italy, Morocco, and Pakistan to travel north and make money (doing the nitty-gritty work Danes refused to do). But all jobs today are scarce, and even Americans—famous and infamous—feel the (usually unspoken) resentment of Danes without jobs.

I guess I'm still in Denmark despite the dirty looks and the job uncertainty because I like Denmark. Or maybe it's because of habit. But I do believe that Denmark is very sane. People wait for traffic lights to change, even at two o'clock in the morning without a car or bike in sight; phones in telephone boxes actually work; salary payments arrive on time; and there are few tax loopholes (that I know of, anyhow). And although, coincidentally, at this moment Danish airport personnel are on strike—you can't land at Kastrup for love or money—strikes, demonstrations, violence, slander, racism, vigilantes, entrapment, television commercials, and similar excitement are exotica for Danes.

In addition, I appreciate the aesthetic touches that Danes value: bringing fresh flowers when you pay a visit, setting the dinner table with colored candles and matching napkins, eating slowly, making eye contact when you say "skål," and having attractive, cozy—the Danish word is "hyggelig"—homes. Danish television has been—that's changing, too—exceptional: a cornucopia of documentaries, nature programs, investigative reporting, and high-quality entertainment, something that reminds me of America's National Public Television. Incidentally, when I showed some Danish friends photos of California lawns made out of plastic grass, they nearly died laughing; synthetic flowers on tombstones also strike them as strange.

How does one get to know a country intimately? By looking at it up close for a long time, although there's no guarantee in that. To be sure, though, brief news items on television can be very misleading. Freak shows make good copy. Danes still kid me about the way Americans are reputed to treat Cabbage Patch dolls like children, and they think vigilantes constitute every second person on American subway systems. This is just as insane an impression as that of Americans who imagine Danish enthusiasm for pornography when, in fact, most pornography is exported because Danes aren't usually willing to waste money on it.

There is one impression others have of Danes, however, which I think approaches a national characteristic. This quality often makes Danes hesitant about making new friendships and pushing ahead in business. It's called *Janteloven*—the term stems from a Danish best seller, and it refers to the ten social commandments. In essence, *Janteloven* commands Danes to drop any hope that they'll get anywhere in life, or that they'll ever amount to anything. Danes are the opposite of the stereotypical pushy American weaned on American Dreams and dollar signs. Danes prefer not to make waves, not to complain about cold coffee in a restaurant, not to raise their voices on a bus. *Janteloven* is one reason Danes rarely call just to chat: the telephone is used to convey a succinct, polite message. Danish friends explain this curtness as unwillingness to disturb others. Personal peace and quiet is highly valued.

And it's just that—the silence—which is becoming rare. A walk on Copenhagen's Strøget, the Walking Street, is now pure cacophony. Videos beep, sex-shop barkers bark, and each store has its own piercing theme song. Today, where the English bookshop, which I loved, used to stand near Copenhagen's Town Hall Square, you can find a fast-food temple with its red plastic furniture, plastic cutlery, and, I'm tempted to say, plastic customers. Denmark is being invaded. Within the last five years, American chain restaurants, Swedish discount supermarkets, and Florida-style shopping malls have made inroads—noisy inroads. I miss my Sunday walks in the King's Forest with nothing more on the agenda than enjoying fresh air, the deer, silence. Stereo portable tape recorders have marred that paradise. Perhaps Denmark has changed rapidly for the worse, or perhaps I remember it as more pristine, quieter, more Danish than it was. Perhaps different things annoy and delight me now than when I was twenty-six. It's impossible to know for sure.

One thing is certain, though. The next time someone asks me what I miss about America—the bagels, the stun-guns, the competition, the excitement—I'll answer, "Not much." It's all here in Denmark. The noisy, commercial side of America have arrived. Another certain thing: when too much of commercial America and loudness and synthetic materials get to Denmark, that will be the last straw.

TENTATIVE CHOICES

Barbara Jensen

I'm living in Denmark rather by accident—I happened to marry a Dane. Looking back, I don't think that I can give any very straightforward answer to the question about why I'm living here rather than in the United States. In fact, I've never decided once and for all to live here rather than there. Instead, I've made a series of tentative choices, which have resulted in my coming here and continuing to live here, and gradually, it has become rather more unlikely—though still not utterly improbable—that I shall return permanently to the United States.

When my husband and I met, we were both students in the United States. At the time we married, we hadn't decided whether we would live in the United States or in Denmark. In any event, we lived in the States for some years before we moved to Denmark. Having spent some very pleasant years as students in the States, we found ourselves in a large and, I thought, depressing city in the Midwest. Neither my husband nor I were particularly happy about our employment situation there, and I loathed the place, so when my husband was offered a job in Denmark, I was happy enough to come along on a trial basis. During the first couple of years we were here, I was rather unhappy and often considered moving back to the United States. Then I found a job that I liked very much, and it encouraged me to stay. Then we had a child and this, too, extended the range of my ties to Danish society. Gradually, my ties to Denmark have become more solid and extensive, my ties to the United States somewhat more attenuated, and the practical difficulties involved in moving back to the States have become distinctly greater. But now and then I still contemplate returning.

As to what I miss about the United States—I mainly miss particular people and particular places, family and friends to whom I feel closer than I do to anyone outside my immediate (nuclear) family here in Denmark, and places I knew and loved when I was young. When I think of the land itself, it is with an abiding affection. It is an incredibly beautiful country with a wild beauty quite unlike the well-tended Danish countryside. On the other hand, I must say, I tend to think of many—though certainly not all—American cities as pockmarks upon the land.

I am sure that there are many things I would miss about Denmark were I to return to the United States. Certainly, I would miss the security and the civility of Danish life. Indeed, the longer I live in Europe, the more puzzling I find it that Americans tolerate the lack of public services and the lack of very basic public safeguards: the shocking lack of public medical care, the deplorable educational standards, the threat that exists to person and property in most urban areas, and so on. Of course, it is difficult to generalize, but overall the level of public morality seems distinctly higher here in Denmark than in the United States. A great effort is made to provide a life of some dignity to the most helpless, vulnerable social groups—the very young, the very old, those who are physically and mentally handicapped, and so on. The results are not perfect in all cases, but in general an effort is made to give all citizens a decent life. I think this is very admirable, and I don't see much evidence of any such commitment in the United States today.

The aspects of Danish and American culture that I value are closely related to other aspects of these cultures that I don't much like. In other words, while there are some things I might like to change in both cultures, I really don't think it is very meaningful to discuss changing isolated bits of a cultural tradition.

Denmark is a small, homogeneous country. The high level of prosperity has tended to foster a high level of public trust. One does not expect to be cheated here—partly because bad reputations, once acquired, are hard to lose. (For example, if one's checking account is overdrawn, one's checks do not at once begin to bounce. The bank where one is known assumes, in our case correctly, that an error may have occurred.) One cannot easily drop out of Danish society and begin life anew. This aspect of Danish society has also, I suppose, helped support the values of the welfare state that I very much admire.

Danish culture, partly because of its homogeneity, has a sort of integrity that is not so easy to come by in the more open, free wheeling culture of the United States—except in culturally isolated religious or ethnic subgroups. Danish culture seems to be of a piece. I haven't seen much of life at the very top or bottom of Danish society, but for wide ranges in between, it is much of a muchness— the porcelain and table linen may be nicer in the upper-middle class home than in the working class home, but the food served for after- noon coffee is much the same, and in more traditional homes, it is served in precisely the same order—buttered buns and richer coffee cake followed by cookies. Life is similar in the town and in the country. Danish culture seems to fit together in its different as- pects—the food, beautifully prepared and served but slightly bland; Danish paintings with their rather muted tones; Danish interior design, sensible, functional, nonflamboyant—all seem to go to- gether. One has one's cultural tradition ready-made here in Den- mark. Danes don't opt in and opt out of alternative traditions in the way many Americans do.

However, being small and homogeneous also has its drawbacks. There is an expansiveness, an openness in American life—a sense (probably in good part factitious, but stimulating nonetheless) that life is open-ended, a myriad of possibilities—not often found here in Denmark. Social life in particular seems more open in the United States than in Denmark. Partly because they move around so much, Americans are more geared to making new friends throughout their lives than Danes are. In Denmark people acquire a small group of friends early in life and confine their social life in later life largely to this small knot of friends and family. Given the small size of the country, there is less danger of losing friends (and perhaps more danger of not being able to free oneself of undesired acquaintances), than in the United States. Whatever the reason, Danes are probably less keen on pursuing new acquaintances than Americans are. The result is that it is more difficult for outsiders to be integrated into Danish society than into American society and also that Danish social life lacks a certain zest.

Both for good and ill, life in Denmark lacks the variety found in the United States. One would be rather hard put to find here either the depths of degradation suffered by the unlucky in the United States or the excitement of life at the top in the United States. Of course, it is an outrageous generalization, but Danes seem more repressed than Americans. Americans quite often strike me as more self-assertive than Danes. Whether this is good or bad, obviously depends on the self that is being asserted.

Partly because of the lack of security in the United States, life there has a cutting edge that is lacking here in Denmark. The insecurity drives many Americans to a life of constant exertion, but they are driven perhaps more by fear of failure than by any distinct positive vision. This, combined with the much larger scale of life in the United States, with its much larger pool of talent to recruit from, tends to foster a superior level of achievement in many occupations. On the other hand, the insecurity also breeds dissatisfaction and a certain selfishness. I've rarely heard even quite successful Americans express much awareness of just how privileged an existence they lead compared with much of humanity, whereas I've often heard Danes say that they were very lucky to be living in Denmark. On the whole, more Danes seem more satisfied with their lives than is the case with Americans. (The reverse side of this is a certain Danish self-satisfaction that many foreigners find infuriating.)

It is difficult to compare the quality of life in Denmark with that in the United States, but on average it is better for a larger proportion of Danes than Americans. Certainly, there is no question as to which country offers a better life for the unfortunate. But for the lucky and the talented who thrive in conditions of uncertainty and who have a taste for constant exertion, for those who are restless and those who have more heroic personalities, life in the United States probably offers challenges and satisfactions not readily found in Denmark.

A PLACE TO FEEL COMFORTABLE

T. Gustafson

Denmark. Why do I live here? Why do I love it in spite of gray, rainy skies and endless winters? Why do I never want to leave even though I love the sun and would thrive in a California climate? Why will California never by my home? Why did I leave America? What caused my disillusionment? Basically I felt like I had to get away because I was so thoroughly disappointed and alienated, an alienation that only increased with each visit after my conscious choice to move to Copenhagen in 1977.

I know now that I could never move back. The road America has been on since even before I emigrated has carried it in a direction that only causes me pain. Much of that pain results from the political climate, but that isn't all. The mentality of the people, their attitudes and values, the things that enrich their lives just aren't the same as what I see as essential to a full and happy life. I feel like an outsider and have apparently always been in the minority. Although I didn't know that in 1968 or 1972, I began to realize it by 1974.

The afternoon I arrived in Madison, Wisconsin, after driving from Seattle, Washington, for three and a half days in a drive-away car, was the day Richard Nixon resigned. That night there was a party in the street on Madison's State Street. I felt like I'd arrived in a town I could feel at home in. But in the two and a half years I lived in Madison, things began to change. By the time I arrived in Denmark in January 1977, I felt pessimistic and disillusioned about my home-land. The trends in the United States in the nine years that have passed have only confirmed my worst fears. What is the United States? What was it then? What has it become? I can't imagine living there, and here are some of the concrete reasons why.

I will divide my feelings and reasons into several categories to make things easier to follow. The Danish status quo in each of the following areas seems to jibe more closely with my own beliefs in a way that has made it almost automatic for me to fit in and feel good about living in Denmark. There was something very nice for me in finding a place where my own viewpoints didn't seem radical, since my own view of myself is not as a radical person. This feeling of fitting in, feeling comfortable and being in agreement with the major-ity, felt wonderful. It made sense to me that my ideas—left of center in America, if not worse!—seemed to be quite usual, not particularly far left, and certainly not subversive in Denmark.

Religion.   Danes are not a particularly religious people, although most are members of the national Lutheran church. Most visit church once a year at Christmas. There are few religious fanatics. Since I am not a member of any church and religion plays no mean-ingful part in my life, this attitude toward the church appeals to me. There is no Jesus freak movement here and only a handful of fundamentalists. Religion is seen more as one's personal relationship to a creator, in the form that one chooses and if one chooses. There is no pressure on you to bring Jesus into your daily life, which I view as a special kind of current American obsession and which I have a very hard time swallowing, maybe because it reminds me more of a naive fatalism than a true commitment to religion.

Sexism.   I sense a truer dedication to equality of the sexes here than in the United States. This dedication to equality has pervaded all layers of the society and has, through political efforts that go back to the sixties, provided families with reasonably priced child care so that women have been able to enter the work force in larger numbers than in any other country in the world. And women have demonstrably proved that they have entered the work force to stay—with, of course, equal wages. Although a recent survey stated that only 40% of all Danish men do share housework and essential child-raising responsibilities with their wives, the topic is so current that even the most conservative newspapers have launched an attack on the chauvinist husbands who have neglected to live up to their half of the bargain.

The question of whether women are actually as intelligent as men is too ridiculous to even be discussed seriously here. (The last time I was in the States, this question was put to debate in all seriousness!)

Custom dictates that everyone change into his or her swimsuit right on the beach here—which doesn't promote gawking, ogling, or other absurdities. In city parks, women sunbathe topless on every single summer day without being attacked—physically or verbally—by passing Danish males. The only oglers I have seen were obviously tourists. The few poor American males I inadvertently led through one Copenhagen park were so overwhelmed by the visual ecstasy of it all that I was embarrassed to be seen with them. Their comments were so gross, their fixation so infantile, and their gesticulations so blatant that I realized once again that the Danish cultural background truly is different. All the Danish men I've questioned on the subject (yes, I've done my own informal survey) have insisted that seing naked female breasts on the beach or in a park was not any kind of sexual turn-on for them. I can only conclude that they have had a different conditioning than their American counterparts, and thank God for that. It definitely is part of what makes Denmark a completely different place to live than the States, where the sexual tension generally strikes me within the first half hour of my arrival. I would also bet that the Bedford gang rape could never happen here.

Personal freedom and safety.   Obviously related to what I have just stated, part of what attracts me to Denmark is that I feel that I have a much greater amount of personal freedom and safety than I would have in America. I do not have to fear going out alone at night, although, of course, rapes do occur here, too. Still, many thousands of women are out alone every evening and demand their right to be safe. The rise in violence of every kind in America shocks and saddens me. Moving to Denmark was in some respects my way of fleeing from the constant, senseless violent spiral that has gripped America since the Vietnam era. Guns, weapons, murders, the ease with which Americans kill each other, the paranoia between people, the tension on city streets, the turmoil and the confusion of it all seemed so pathetic, inhuman, revolting, and unfathomable. Moving to Denmark was like escaping to a humane haven where the occasional murder still makes front page headlines. American friends tell me that they've learned to live with the violence or that they've just sort of become immune to it. Maybe I'm a chicken, but I just never could get used to it and my own personal fear of it definitely played a part in my wanting to leave the United States and head for a more civilized country.

I would, however, be naive to pretend that violent crime has not increased in the eight years that I've lived here. Unfortunately, it has. Yet I am confident that it will never reach the proportions that are seen in the United States today, partly because of the strict Danish antihandgun laws.

Political and social systems.   More than once, Americans have asked what it is like to live in a socialist country. This to me is an example of Americans' political ignorance. Denmark is a so-called social democracy. (In fact, the representation in its unicameral parliament is much more proportional than in any governing body in the United States. At the present time, we have a Conservative coalition government.) Denmark is also a capitalist country with free enterprise and private ownership of property—the things that we normally associate with nonsocialist countries. We pay slightly higher taxes than the average American (our wages are also higher), and for those taxes we receive, among other things, free education from kindergarten through the higher education system; free national health insurance including free medical and hospital care; subsidized dental care for adults and free dental care for children; a highly subsidized system of child care programs, home nurse programs, and in-home care for the elderly as well as rest homes and nursing homes; a careful system of nationalized welfare designed to prevent anyone from having to move from their home or be in need of food or clothing in the event of unemployment, sickness, or accident.

For our taxes, however, we do not get a huge defense budget. Denmark is a member of NATO and is regularly criticized by this organization for not doing enough and living up to its end of the bargain. So far, Denmark has no missiles deployed on its territory, and the majority of the population opposes any such deployment. Nor are there any atomic energy plants producing energy for the public utility system here.

Competition, television, and creativity.   I find Americans more competitive than Danes, probably because American history is replete with stories based on the "every man for himself" motto. The fittest, the survivors, the champions, and the heroes are rewarded, while the weak, the poor, and the down-and-out are largely ignored. Americans are "fighters" and "go-getters," while Danes are more tuned to solidarity. In these years of unemployment with the current influx of refugees from Iran, among other places, in addition to the population of guest workers from Turkey and other countries, Danish open-mindedness is being put to the test. The vocal racism of the most right-wing party in Denmark has stunned me and has been the most disappointing jolt in the years I've lived here, but it is not the attitude of the majority.

Americans differ from Danes in their relationship to entertainment and to the television world that is instantly available round-the-clock to Americans. Danes do not yet have this complication in their lives since the one national television station comes on in the late afternoon and goes off the air again at around midnight. (The first two experiments with cable television have just recently begun in the greater Copenhagen area.) Because of this alone, viewing is limited and Danish television is not contaminated by commercials. These facts alone mean that television is not the main source of national humor, nor are programs or commercials the source of immense amounts of new slang, as is the case in America. Having not been an American television viewer for more than eight years, I have to have American jokes and humor explained to me when I visit.

I also think that there is an awareness here that one has and ought to keep active mentally and not become a television idiot in one's free time. People take more walks, do more things together as a family, enjoy more of the simpler things in life, and life is less complicated. Few families have more than one car, and maybe people take things a little easier, finding more time to be together and to share daily experiences. If it is true that there is more creativity here—and I tend to think that there is—maybe these are part of the explanation. Children are allowed to and encouraged to be creative, and adults too are encouraged to be more creative than in America, basically because the society, being less rigid and conservative, allows more areas where creativity can thrive and flourish.

Some of my American friends who live here feel that Denmark lacks some sense of energy that they feel when they are in the United States. They are not sure how to define this energy or what it actually consists of. I am convinced that the same energy levels exist here but that people channel and express this energy in quite different ways. Competitiveness is not here to the same extent; there is more caring for others and more room for loyalty and solid, long-lasting friendships. I feel that Danes are much less superficial than average Americans, and my experience is that they invest great energy in friendships that last a long time. My American friends have not been able to live up to that, even most of the very best of them—a true disappointment to me.

A big part of traditional Danish creativity is, as I see it, based on the idea of making it yourself, instead of buying it. Crafts such as knitting, crocheting, sewing, and making decorations of paper for Christmas and Easter are extremely popular. Shopping is definitely less of a pastime and a family outing since stores simply aren't open on weekends after 2:00 P.M. on Saturdays or on weekdays after 5:30 P.M. Going for a Sunday walk demands being more creative than driving to the nearest shopping center and browsing for two hours. The physical framework for everyday life can force one to think more creatively. I know that if I were in the United States, I would spend more hours shopping than I do here, only because I could go into stores virtually around the clock.

Views toward children and the elderly.   Finally, I feel that children and the elderly are viewed and treated as real people here, that there is respect for their rights and abilities. I hope that is the case in the United States, too.

DENMARK: THE MAGIC OF THE CHILD
Scott Churchill Leland

I don't know that I consider myself an expatriate exactly; I came to Denmark to visit a friend I'd met in England and just stayed on— for years. The pastry tasted so good, and the women were so sexful and wholesome.

I think America is essentially a young country still in its adolescence—rushing around madly trying on the latest styles, eating junk food, driving too fast, generally making trouble for its neighbors, showing off its physical strength—still basically insecure and not very educated yet.

Denmark is grown-up and settled down with some sensible rules for living.

The quality of life in Denmark is better and so is the bread—it has some nutrition in it and it tastes good. I wouldn't dream of knocking the Washington Monument or Disneyland. Interestingly, the biggest-selling magazine in Denmark is the weekly Donald Duck comic book—you can even see adults on the local train reading it, sitting next to a well-dressed grandmother smoking a cigar. And, yes, the women don't wear bras—it's an unnecessary additive to the natural life.

I guess most of the more cosmopolitan Danes living in the capital city, Copenhagen, still have an uncle or a cousin working on a farm somewhere on the peninsula of Jutland. It is a provincial country, but at the same time it has some of the most beautiful ballet dancing in the world. Copenhagen is charming—a lovely city, really, with one of the lowest crime rates in the world. The citizens have an innate sense of honesty and ethics. There is even a law that if you see someone in trouble on the street and don't help him, you can be arrested—it wouldn't work in New York City.

One of the national sports is badminton—light and free, an indoor sport. The Danes share the world championship matches with the Japanese and Indonesians.

There is a premium on space in Denmark—it can take months or years to find an apartment. Every inch of space is owned by someone. In America two-thirds of the country is still uninhabited forest; Indians may still be lurking in the backyard. Half of the families in the United States own a firearm (which might account for the high crime rate), but the gun-toting cowboys have been dead now for at least two generations.

There is a popular song in Denmark: "Danish soldiers have their pockets full of tomatoes." To give to the pretty farm girls, I guess. Sex is more fun than war.

In Denmark there is "child power," not unlike "flower power." Children are the center of attention and are even looked up to. In America, children are treated more like dogs who make messes and should be controlled, like dolls who look nice but don't understand English, or like robots who should be placed in front of the television and forgotten. In Denmark, children are treated as people, and their magical universes of fantasy and innocence are respected and loved.

A MATTER OF DEGREES
Bill Heinrich

Saying farewell to the American way of life is probably the easiest aspect of moving to Denmark. But actually forgetting American television, American sports, American fast-food chains, let alone one's identity as an American, is next to impossible.

Flying across the Atlantic does not end with a mere change of perspective. If an American lives in Denmark permanently, he or she undergoes a redefinition of personal values and priorities. The process is subtle. It almost inevitably begins with the question, which country—the United States or Denmark—offers a better quality of life? Because there is no clear-cut answer and because Americans seem to have an inbred urge to rank people and countries, a comparison of the two countries is probably the topic most commonly discussed whenever you find two or more Americans together in Denmark.

How one adjusts to Denmark, of course, depends upon many things, particularly why one came here. In my case, it wasn't too difficult to leave the United States and join my Danish wife here in Denmark. I was glad to get away from the midwestern rednecks with their pickup trucks and "America—love it or leave it" bumper stickers. I found the American Dream to be hollow and, in most cases, the exception, not the rule. Thoreau's statement that the mass of men lead lives of quiet desperation seemed a truism that was particularly applicable to America.

Thus, with no ambition of ever becoming a yuppie, I booked my flight to Denmark with little or no hesitation. In short, the idea of living in a modern welfare state—even with its higher taxes and lower pay—seemed appealing. I looked forward to living in a country where a majority of the population and the government are antinuclear—they refuse to allow nuclear weapons and they refuse to build nuclear energy plants. It all seemed so idyllic.

In retrospect, I must admit that I overemphasized the role that politics and public institutions have in determining the quality of life. While governmental institutions and private corporations may dominate world power and, indeed, shape and reflect a society's ideology, they are not directly involved in the interaction between people. And it is primarily the interaction between individuals that determines the quality of life (assuming, though, that a population's basic needs are first met).

Nonetheless, it's quite natural for a newly arrived American to focus on the public institutions. One cannot help but be impressed by the degree to which Danes have embodied the notion of equal opportunity in their institutions. They certainly have been more successful than Americans. All Danes—regardless of birth or income—have equal access to free health care, free university education, and a myriad of social programs designed to assist families in need. Unemployment does not bring havoc to the family, and sickness does not wipe out a life's savings.

It is noteworthy that Danish institutions have been advanced—or at least not deterred—by the Danish population's homogeneity. And this homogeneity has contributed to the evolvement of Danish collectivism. Although Danes have strong isolationist tendencies in world politics, they believe in collectivism in domestic matters. Unlike pluralistic America with all its competing ethnic, racial, and religious groups, Denmark is a nation of WASPs (almost all Danes have been brought up Lutheran), who share an almost identical cultural heritage. Danish society is not plagued by the schisms that mark American society. Danes are less prone to classify other Danes into subgroups that challenge their own legitimacy. Antisemitism seems almost nonexistent. Communists are just as Danish as Conservatives. I have yet to see a "Denmark—love it or leave it" bumper sticker on a pickup or a Volvo.

While Americans seem to thrive on adversity and litigation, medical malpractice suits, for example, are still relatively rare in Denmark. Although the Danish legal system does not allow the plaintiff's attorney a percentage, there appears to be a real hesitation on the part of most Danes to instigate a lawsuit against a fellow Dane.

Interestingly, many of the Danish welfare institutions, such as the health care system and the unemployment benefit program, are premised upon mutual self-help and not aid to the poor. The distinction is critical because it reflects their underlying ideology or belief that survival through hard times depends upon cooperation—not competition.

This faith in cooperation forms, in turn, the groundwork for an essential feature of Danish life: security. Never in my life have I felt the security I do now. I do not believe it's merely attributable to my marital status, job, or living conditions. I believe that Danes consciously and deliberately attempt to construct an environment that reinforces a feeling of security.

In common parlance this sense of security manifests itself in the frequent use of the phrase *Tag det stille og roligt* (Take it easy). The phrase is more than just a slogan or a byword; it's a sincere and serious proposal. It's mentioned in all aspects of life—in sports, at home, on the tennis court, and even at work.

Another example of the Danes' search for security is their sense of orderliness and quality. It's no accident that roads and highways are free of litter and that the Danish landscape appears almost mani-cured. Although most Danes may take it easy at their jobs, they are generally perfectionists when it comes to maintaining their home and garden. It must be almost impossible to grow up in Denmark and not develop some opinion about interior and exterior design.

Danes do not stop, however, at constructing an orderly physical environment. They have developed rituals that aim at creating an atmosphere of intimacy. When an occasion is characterized by this intimacy, Danes say it is *hyggeligt*. Though *hyggeligt* is commonly translated to mean cozy, it connotes, actually, a sense of security that allows an atmosphere of intimacy to be nurtured. Danes blend candles, decorations, food, song, and patterns of behavior fixed by tradition to instill in their guests the desired feeling: security. Like-wise, the guests act out their parts as defined by custom. It's an art developed into a set of expected rituals, exercised by both the host and the guest.

I am, of course, generalizing and no reader should construe that what I'm writing applies to all Danes. Nonetheless, I believe it's accurate to characterize the Danish desire for security as the underly-ing motive for many of their behaviors and cultural traits. Despite their own little world in the North, Danes are quite aware that the outside world may not have the same set of priorities. Their isolationism and general reluctance to integrate with continental Europe stems, in large part, from a fear of losing control (sovereignty) and, hence, security should they join a European commonwealth.

Occasionally, an event occurs that shocks their world of secure, well-built homes and fixed rituals. An example is the recent ugly and senseless murder of Olaf Palme, Sweden's prime minister. One expects political assassinations to occur everywhere else but not in the North, where freedom, peace, and security are so highly valued. The murder struck deep. It was not just another senseless assassination of a man of peace.

Portrayal of the Danish quality of life cannot, however, rest solely upon the Danish egalitarian institutions and Danes' deliberate attempt to create a secure environment. I expect that I'm typical of the many Americans who come to live in Denmark in that beautiful homes, beautiful people, a beautiful landscape, and a safety net are alone inadequate for a good life.

Possibly because I'm American, I've come to expect a stimulating, high-energy environment. I appreciate randomness, spontaneity, energy, and a degree of anarchy. "It's better to burn out than die," as a rock star once sang. Possibly a remnant of the frontier spirit, most Americans still possess a deep-seated disdain for rules and bureaucracy (despite the pervasive dominance of the modern corporation). Comedian David Letterman is so popular because of his rowdy, unpredictable, contemptuous humor. Although a planned evening at the movies is nice, a spontaneous outing to the beach, a park, the tennis courts, McDonald's, or an all-night grocery can be nirvana.

Thus, for an American brought up on Wonder Bread, American television and the hectic pace of life, security—Danish security—is a double-edged sword. In contrast to the rat race of America that begins at birth (or even before for the test-tube babies of Nobel Laureats), a desperate soul can take it easy, unwind, and even find security in Denmark. But the same security that calms the soul, unfortunately, dampens spontaneity. The rituals that are charming to the newcomer act restrictively on the permanent resident.

It's not just that birthday parties held in Copenhagen, Aalborg, Aarhus, and Odense are nearly identical, the problem is that rituals are narrowly prescribed. Deviation from the norm is unacceptable. In short, predictability is the quintessence of acceptability. At Christmas, thou shalt dance around the Christmas tree. At lunch, thou shalt eat herring first and with a slice of rye bread. At dinner, thou shalt light the candles. Thou shalt not rush. "Take it easy" is the first commandment.

One is expected—in all senses of the word—to behave in the prescribed way. Danes have an expression that describes their indignation when someone tries to rock the boat. They say, "Man kan ikke være bekendt" (One cannot be known). It's a strong statement. It's almost a moral condemnation. Luckily, as an American, I can escape the condemnation, but not the indignation.

Maybe it's the deterring influence of a long, cold, dark winter, but planning most often substitutes for spontaneity. "Plan ahead" must be the Danish motto. Monday night is Spanish lessons, Tuesday is gymnastics, Wednesday is the movies. On Thursday one stays at home and has it *hyggeligt*. One shops on Friday (it may be the only night the stores are open late). On Saturday one does the yard work and on Sunday one reads the newspaper and watches "Dynasty" and the evening news on television.

Occasionally, though, spontaneity breaks through all the planning. Coincidentally or not, it seems to happen most when it gets warm. There are usually a few summer evenings where there's an electricity in the air. It's as if one can see and feel the northern lights. The walking streets fill with people. Life becomes suddenly carefree. There's a jovial warmth. Danes drinking their Tuborg or Carlsberg beer join for a song. Clothes and colors seem so varied and merry. Couples hold hands and eat their soft ice cream. Children run loose with pockets filled with candy. At those rare moments both the security and the spontaneity of life in Denmark cannot be exceeded.

Even more than the Danish obsession with planning, the cultural trait most at odds with the American temperament is the Danish resentful envy of almost anyone who achieves and climbs to the top. This envy is so well known and pervasive that Danes have given it legal status: they call it "Jante's Law." In everyday language, "Jante's Law" is expressed in sentences like, "Don't think you're anybody special," "Don't think you're any smarter than we are," "Don't think you're any better," "Don't think you can laugh at us," and, "Don't think you can teach us anything." In practice it's egalitarianism at its worst. It's tyranny by the majority. The particular problem with "Jante's Law" is that it creates an almost irrefutable presumption that an achiever, simply because he or she excels, has a superiority complex. The presumption, standing alone, would not be so serious, but ostracism is the social consequence. "Jante's Law" places Danish leaders among some of the world's loneliest. It seeks equality not by lifting the majority but by threatening those who wish to achieve with the stigma of superiority and social ostracism.

Because both the United States and Denmark are affluent societies with a high degree of political freedom, discussion of the quality of life assumes a different nature than if one were comparing the United States and an impoverished third world country or a country with authoritarian rule. One can assume that most basic human needs must first be met. One can also assume that the political system must protect certain natural rights and ensure franchisement and equal representation for all its citizens. Therefore, the notion of the quality of life becomes both more abstract and more exacting when one is comparing the United States and Denmark. A simple and concrete act of providing food will not result in the American or Danish recipient pronouncing that he now has a good life. Fortunately or unfortunately, we are more demanding precisely because we are so privileged.

Since one's basic needs are satisfied, quality becomes a question of security, self-realization, and interraction with one's environment. While I have generalized much about both America and Denmark in this essay, I should also point out that I have considerable freedom in both countries to determine who my friends and associates are—for it is the quality of my interractions with them that is the primary determinant of my well-being.

The bottom line is that a choice between the United States and Denmark is not a choice between security and spontaneity. The difference between the United States and Denmark is a matter of degrees. One can very well find oneself in a rut in the United States or in a burst of tradition-breaking behavior in Denmark. But if American television, American sports, American fast-food chains, and the American way of life are dear to one's heart, then one should critically evaluate moving to Denmark before coming.

Contributors

Ellen Bick Meier graduated from the School for Performing Arts in New York City and received an M.A. from Johns Hopkins University. She lives in Copenhagen, teaches at Blaagaard State College, and is book and theater critic for the Danish national newspaper *Information*. She has published four books on a variety of subjects.

Barbara Jensen moved to Denmark in 1976. She is a teacher on the island of Fyn.

T. Gustafson holds an M.A. in Scandinavian Languages and Literatures from the University of Wisconsin. She is married to a Dane, has one child, and has lived in Denmark since 1977.

Scott Churchill Leland was born in Springfield, Massachusetts, in 1937. He attended Amherst College and the University of Massachusetts and has won several prizes for his poetry. He married Vita, who is Danish, and lives with her in Copenhagen.

Bill Heinrich was born in 1957 in Missouri and was educated at the University of Missouri at Columbia, receiving an A.B. in sociology, political science, and biology, followed by a J.D. degree. He has traveled widely and worked at a number of jobs. He now lives in Odense.

4

Limbo

In the strict sense of the word, limbo is not entirely appropriate to describe the condition of most of the Americans who live in Denmark, for they certainly do not always feel that they live in "a place or condition of neglect or oblivion to which unwanted things or persons are relegated." Nevertheless, the way we use the term popularly, to indicate an in-between, indefinite place is certainly adequate to describe how Americans in Denmark often feel. As Greg Stephenson says in his essay, "Living here for me is both a sort of refuge and a sort of banishment." These essays most clearly speak to that issue.

BIOS XENIKON BLUES

Gregory Stephenson

Riding on a commuter train in Copenhagen one day not long ago, reading a book, I came across a phrase from Aristotle pertaining to the state of foreigners and exiles: *bios xenikon*—the life of a stranger. I reflected how the phrase fit my own life and I felt both pride and sadness.

51

In the spring of 1960 when I was in the seventh grade, I determined to live in Europe. At the time, all I knew about Europe was derived from a few films and novels and my grade school geography lessons, but it seemed to me so romantic, so exotic, so magical and mysterious compared to the flat, dry landscape of tract homes and the bland, sunblinded suburbs of west Phoenix, Arizona, where I lived. But I think that the deepest reason for my attraction to Europe was my sense of myself as a misfit (neither a jock nor a hood, neither a grind nor a wimp nor a nerd, etc.) and the idea that in Europe, a stranger among strangers, this condition would somehow be resolved or alleviated.

During my high school years, as my sense of alienation grew more acute and as I read further and more widely, I learned that among disaffected, alienated Americans, Europe was considered the sphere of true taste and values and the realm of a more authentic life, and that for decades, Americans had expatriated themselves to Europe in flight from the puritanism, provincialism, pragmatism, and materialism of their native land. From *Evergreen Review, Playboy, National Geographic,* and foreign films, I learned that Europe (especially Scandinavia) was socially and sexually progressive and politically liberal, that culture and the arts were esteemed there, and that a measure of human mercy was embodied in such institutions as the penal system, national health insurance, and other features of social democracy or the welfare state that so horrified Americans.

During my last two years of high school, I worked evenings and weekends at a grocery store and saved my money to go to Europe. In June of 1965, just a few days after my high school graduation, I set off with a friend for the promised land of my soul. Landing in Copenhagen, we traveled during the next four months through Germany, Holland, Belgium, France, and Spain, and then returned to Denmark again, crossing also to Sweden. It was the Scandinavian countries that most impressed me with their quality of life, their cleanness, their honesty and humanity, their lack of prudery and aggressiveness. When I left for the States, I vowed that I would return to Denmark the following year to live there on a permanent basis.

Unfortunately, due to complications with the Selective Service and involvement with the military, I was not able to return to Denmark until September 1972. In the meantime, I had married a Danish woman, Birgit, whom I'd met on my trip in 1965. Upon our return, we settled in Odense, Birgit's hometown, and lived there until April 1980, when we moved to Tempe, Arizona, for sixteen months, then returned again to Denmark in September 1981, settling first in Charlottenlund and finally in Copenhagen, where we presently reside.

At this writing, then, I have lived in Denmark for a total of nearly eleven years. I have no immediate plans to return to the United States, though I would like to try to do so again if I could find suitable employment there. I continue to believe that Denmark is one of the two or three most civilized countries in the world. (The United States, in my view, and according to various quality of life ratings, is about tenth or twelfth in rank among civilized countries.) And I mean *civilized* in the best sense of the word—not effete or decadent, but sensible, sane, humane. The Danish welfare system and ideal of social democracy provide a workable synthesis of capitalism and socialism and should serve as a model to the world.

During our recent sixteen-month stay in the United States, my wife and I were frequently dismayed and appalled at the climate of economic exploitation that continues to exist at all levels: employer-employee relations (maximum work for minimum wages); landlord-tenant relations, the utter insufficiency of the American "security net" of social welfare legislation, and the psychological degradation of the poor and unfortunate. How often we observed practices that were illegal or inconceivable in Denmark. One image out of many continues to haunt me: the sight of a legless beggar shuffling on his stumps down a dirt road in south Phoenix. In Denmark, the man would have had a pension, a wheelchair, and the street would have been paved.

Let me check, at this point, what may seem to be an unrelievedly negative tone to my depiction of the United States and a corresponding idealization of Denmark. There is much that I admire, much that I love and value in the United States, and there are a number of things here of which I disapprove. (I am frequently in the position here of defending and explaining aspects of the United States to Europeans.) Nor have I, since my adolescence, credited the notion that Europe is the realm of true taste and values and authentic life, whereas the United States is afflicted by puritanism, provincialism, and materialism. But the aspects of European life that I would wish my country to adopt are generally things that could easily be made into law and put into practice; while those features of the United States that I most esteem and that I might wish incorporated into European life (such as the free style, cultural vitality, and pluralism of America) are qualities that would be much more difficult (if at all possible) to transplant.

The following are some credits and debits (very subjective, of course) concerning Danish society.

There seems to be significantly less competitive masculine aggressiveness here than in the States. Danish males permit themselves forms of behavior that would be considered unmasculine in the United States. The relationship between the sexes is characterized here by far more ease and ordinary friendliness than in the United States; there is much more contact and exchange on a nonerotic, nonsexist basis. Policemen here are not menacing presences (they are generally unarmed as well). I have seen policemen reason with abusive, aggressive drunks rather than assaulting or arresting them. There is a general tendency on the part of persons in a position of authority here—whether teachers, train conductors, bus drivers, or parents—to avoid an inflexible stance against an adversary, one that allows the adversary no dignified choice but to assume an equally inflexible stance. Disputes are generally kept on a human level, defused short of insult or violence. In this same regard, there is a greater degree of common gentleness here, an avoidance of violent rage or confrontation. There is more social naturalness, more leniency and latitude extended: girls walk hand in hand with each other on the streets without being thought to be Lesbians; nudity and seminudity are far more prevalent and accepted; various manifestations of sexualtiy are subject to far less intolerance and hysteria. (I remember that in Odense, on the street where we lived, there was a "massage clinic" less than thirty yards from a grade school. The children passed by it morning and afternoon. This would be inconceivable in the United States.)

Danes tend to be introverted and reserved, sometimes to a degree that suggests aloofness or indifference. Danes are far less religious than people of other nations. Their attitude toward spiritual matters is most often outright skepticism or contemptuous dismissal. Their lives lack a metaphysical dimension. Danish intellectuals tend towards a complacent smugness, a dogmatic self-righteousness (especially concerning political theories and issues) that often reflects a remarkable shallowness of thought. Intellectual fashions, orthodoxies, and radically stereotypical thinking seem more pronounced among Danish than American intellectuals. (Some examples are vehement denunciation of the United States and uncritical admiration for Albania, Cuba, or North Korea.)

The experience of being an expatriate has been, and continues to be, an ambiguous one for me. I have often felt lonely and isolated here. I have turned the radio dial on winter nights hoping to hear an English-speaking voice, and I have longed to talk with someone who shares my language and experience (all the trivial things such as Kool-Aid, Quaker Oats, rock and roll, old television commercials; all the emblems and histories and recognized phrases or memories, the flotsam and jetsam of shared culture). I've felt frustrated in trying to obtain particular books and journals relevant to my research. I've resisted the thought of growing old here, an old foreigner in a foreign land. I've noticed that my night dreams are almost exclusively of past or projected experiences in the United States.

But I've exulted in the uniqueness of experiences that I have had here: knowing myself to be the only foreigner at certain gatherings or events; talking with farmers, old ladies, shopkeepers in their own tongue. I've felt privileged to read books in Danish or to overhear conversations, to see Danish cityscapes and landscapes. As a foreigner, there can be a special thrill to quite ordinary experiences, an intensity, a heightening of feeling, a sense of adventure to everyday life. In this sense, my seventh grade dream of a romantic, exotic, magical Europe has often been fulfilled.

In common with the waves of American expatriates who have come to Europe before me, I have learned that to live abroad for an extended period of time involves a process of self-discovery that may be quite different from that which was anticipated. Living in a foreign land has taught me how essentially American I am and how much I value my Americanness. I have realized that ultimately, I am far less alienated from my native country and from my compatriots than I formerly felt myself to be and far less than I would have been had I remained there in the sort of interior exile that many disaffected Americans maintain. ("Oh! he who has never been afar," wrote Herman Melville in *Redburn*, "let him once go from home, to know what home is.")

And yet, I can't dismiss or disregard the degree of estrangement and the conflict of values that continues to remain between myself and American society, because the consequences for me are appreciable in psychic and material terms. That is to say that I am unable to find employment in America doing the kind of work I find meaningful and for which I'm suited: teaching. It is obviously an indication of American social values that those who embrace the humanities, the moral and spiritual values, are unemployed or working at menial jobs, while those who pursue technological and material interests are rewarded with jobs. To take a job in industry or some other commercial enterprise (as I've done in the past) would represent to me, at a personal and ideological level, not merely compromise but capitulation.

Very probably, living in Denmark has stimulated and determined the direction of my intellectual and creative pursuits in the past decade. Certainly, it has provided me with the leisure (because of the enlightened Danish system of unemployment insurance) to undertake research and to write. The direction that my reading and writing has taken is toward the understanding of American thought and experience. I read and write criticism of American authors and poets, seeking my identity and true homeland in the spirit of American literature, hoping that, in my small way, I may aid the struggle to redeem "the lost America of love" (as Allen Ginsberg calls it in "A Supermarket in California").

In the meantime and for the duration, however long that may prove to be, I remain here, grateful for the generous hospitality of my host country, often lonesome for the deeper attractions of my home country. I feel ambivalent and tentative; living here for me is both a sort of refuge and a sort of banishment. In short, I got a case of them old bios xenikon blues (pass the bottle, Aristotle)—them old funky, mean and low-down, bad-ass bios xenikon blues.

AN AMERICAN ON BORNHOLM

Barbara Brændgaard

Sitting alone in my living room knitting, I can look out onto the snow-covered square, which, except for a few cars and television antennas, must look almost the same as it did one hundred years ago when my house was built, with red brick walls and low barn-red and ochre half-timber houses crouching right next to the cobblestoned streets. The little square, which then was probably filled with activity in front of the merchant's buildings, is now a quiet garden, where old people like to sit in the summer, enjoying a cake from the nearby baker while children play games among the flower beds.

My parents, sister, and brother are perhaps also looking out on snow, but they all live isolated in the forests of Maine. I live in the thriving town of Rønne with fifteen thousand habitants on the Danish island of Bornholm in the middle of the Baltic Sea.

"All alone with nothing to do . . . entirely surrounded by water," complained Piglet in E. E. Milnes' *Winnie the Pooh*, but that is scarcely my problem. In a small community there is always a need for people who want to do something, so I am the treasurer of my local party organization. I was a candidate for town council. I sing in a chorus and can, if I want, go to numerous meetings, concerts, or theatrical productions, both amateur and professional, that my American family must drive many miles to go to. If I want to go to something "out on the island" away from Rønne, I can take one of the buses that run every hour, so I have no car and don't want one. Copenhagen is just a night's sail away or a half an hour by plane, so even the delights of the capitol are close by.

But how did I happen to land here on this little island, alone? Like many generations of my family before me (who traveled from England and Germany to America, from California to New Jersey and back again, and finally to the woods of Maine), I came here because I was curious and because I wanted to try something new. I didn't go to Bornholm right away, though, but to Copenhagen—the only place I'd ever heard of in Denmark. Like so many before me I fell in love and then married a Dane. After three years study in North Carolina, we returned, with almost completed Ph.D.'s, to Denmark, partly because my husband thought he could get a job here (he didn't get a permanent one, though, for many years), but also because we figured that Denmark was one of the most peaceful places in the world (the year being 1972 when America was involved in Vietnam and Watergate) and if he didn't get a job, it would be easier to be unemployed here, with the well-developed Danish social services.

To improve my job prospects, I took a Danish master's degree in German and English, only to discover that Denmark didn't think it needed people in the humanities anymore, a problem that also existed in the States at that time.

Although the social services kept us physically comfortable, I became painfully aware that I desperately needed a job in order to be mentally comfortable. Probably because of my difficult situation, our marriage deteriorated rapidly, so in 1980 I took the only job I could find, leaving our then seven-year-old daughter Hanne with her father in Aalborg and taking ten-year-old Pelle with me to Bornholm, where I had managed to capture the last job in Denmark teaching German and English—at the island's only gymnasium (university preparatory high school).

At that point I certainly considered moving back to the States, but it would have meant being prohibitively far away from my daughter. Otherwise, I suppose I would have, as there was really nothing else to keep me. Recently the thought has occurred to me again in connection with Pelle's plans to spend next year in Maine living with my parents and going to high school. But somehow I almost feel too old to try to get into teaching in the American school system.

I feel very alone now and have felt so most of the time I have lived in Denmark. It is another sort of isolation than what my parents have living in their forest. When I walk into town I often greet numerous people, colleagues, students, fellow politicians, neighbors, and members of various organizations and interest groups I am involved in. When the telephone or doorbell rings, however, it is either for my son or someone with a particular message, not just someone calling for a chat. When I have problems I have several people I can turn to, but none of them ever asks for help. Weekends I spend with my friend but only rarely are we together with other people as well, although he has several friends he sometimes is with—without me—during the week. Even my friend often corrects my Danish grammar or regards certain of my actions as strange, thereby letting me know that he doesn't consider me quite normal.

Most Danes seem to have one very good friend, with no one else really being important to them, even though, as I said, they are perfectly willing to be helpful if asked. I remember being rather astonished soon after moving back to Denmark to hear a woman say she scarcely knew any of her neighbors, for "just because we're neighbors doesn't mean we have anything in common." My own experience in the States was more often that one had much in common with one's neighbors, if for no other reason than gardens, yards, and kids. Danes are very reluctant to move from their hometowns, I assume because they just aren't accustomed to making friends as easily as Americans do.

I have recently been feeling more and more cramped in my job, where I teach English and German to teenagers who are relatively fluent in those languages, as they have had the former for five years and the latter for three years before entering the gymnasium. I feel I have little opportunity to be creative in my work. Even though the system is presumably more flexible than in an American high school (my only experience there is my own schooling twenty-five years ago), as we can pretty much choose what texts we want to use (among those the school happens to have), I often feel great hindrances on my freedom of choice because the students are also party to deciding on the year's reading materials. Danish children are brought up very democratically, and they are permitted to make many choices from an early age. Unfortunately they quite often disagree, not only with me but with each other, so that it is hard to get them to work together on a text they don't think they will like. Texts tend to be about the students themselves, as I find it difficult to interest them in new horizons.

As a teacher I feel I am only there to encourage my students to speak and write. They are not terribly interested in my viewpoints, so I rarely express them. The teaching is rather Socratic—I ask leading questions to draw out what they know or think about a text. Very rarely do I give a lecture, and if I do, no one dreams of taking notes. It is their own opinion that counts. Consequently, I have completely lost touch with most of what I studied for many years, and I only rarely get inspired to try a new approach to a text, as it is completely lost on the students as soon as the class is over. I seem to remember that we took many notes, both in high school and college, and considered our teachers authorities in their fields. Danish students have been taught to think independently, which is certainly very important and which is a skill many American students seem to lack, but they are not very well trained in assimilating knowledge and ideas that others have worked out before them. I have been reminded that my present students are the children of the rebellious "68-ers" and that the grade school curriculum, too, was greatly influenced by their rather misguided ideas on democracy, whereby everyone was to have an equal say in everything. In a few years, the tides should turn, so it might be easier to be a teacher again.

In a sense, the attitude of "I'll do it my way" pervades Danish society. Time and again I have seen Danes working out a "new" way to do something that has been used for numerous years (and sometimes later rejected) in, for example, America. I remember my horror at seeing the enormous new town, Albertslund, outside Copenhagen, which seemed to make all the dreadful mistakes of Levittown. It consisted of rows of identical houses, with each different type in its own separate enclave and with no attempt to vary the houses within a group by anything other than a bit of paint or mirror imaging.

Many years after Dr. Spock's recantation, parents here are still dreadfully afraid of correcting their children for fear of disturbing them mentally. This fear, moreover, affects the children's upbringing so that many children scarcely know what is right and wrong in, among other things, group relations. The problem is compounded by the fact that the parents, who are both working, have little time or energy to be with their children in their spare time. It is often much easier to do things yourself than to try to get children to learn how to do their part in the household. This means that by the time the children reach school, they have no respect for the authority of a teacher, who then has the almost impossible task of teaching them to sit still, listen, and do what is expected of them. Children in school can go off to the rest rooms freely without having to ask, but they use the rest rooms as an excuse to leave the classroom whenever they feel like it, which can be quite disturbing to the class and to the child's learning process.

I am an active Social Democrat because it seems to me that a more or less socialistic welfare system is appropriate for Denmark. I find many aspects of this system praiseworthy: free education and medical care, government-supported sick pay, unemployment insurance, and public support of the arts. In fact, the people expect these services, so that not even a Conservative government would privatize as much as in America, even though the current government is making several attempts in that direction.

Americans do not expect much nationalization and seem to manage to provide the same services to almost everyone through various, generally private, sources, with the government only taking over when the private resources or interest are lacking. I feel that in the States, public concern for all citizens prompts doctors to charge more for their services to some patients in order to be able to serve others for very little (which Danes simply cannot understand), and it prompts private universities to seek out needy students for special scholarships, which are often paid for by funds from industry. In Denmark everyone has an equal opportunity to get a scholarship, or government loan, but the amounts are so low that many students have to find extra employment to live on while they study.

The Danes, like most Europeans, have simply been accustomed to having someone (a feudal lord) take care of them in return for other services. People went to America to escape such paternalism, and they made the country what it is through individualism and mutual self-help. The Danish and American concepts are so incompatible that the American way wouldn't work here (as present government attempts show) and the Danish way wouldn't be accepted in America.

In some ways the assumption that the government will solve

all problems leads to some very unimaginative results in Denmark. The many budgetary cuts of recent years have lead mostly to smaller welfare checks, schools that don't function as well as they used to (even though Denmark prides itself on having the world's best school system), a poorly paid public sector, and worst of all, long waiting lists for the hospitals, which means that old people in particular who are no longer in the work force have to wait many painful months or even years for cataract or hip operations. I suspect private enterprise in America often steps in where government leaves off, providing more innovative solutions.

Recently in school, a student asked me how to translate the Danish expression "Jante's law," as it wasn't in her dictionary. I finally concluded that it couldn't be translated, because the concept doesn't exist in America. The "law" pronounces that you shouldn't think you're better than other people. A somewhat related American concept, is "keeping up with the Joneses." If neighbors in Denmark get a new car, you immediately figure they cheated someone to be able to have enough money to get it, with the easiest way to cheat being through taxes in which case they've cheated everyone. In America you go out and buy an even bigger car, which might mean having to work harder to be able to do it.

Strangely enough, although the Danes maintain group mediocrity through "Jante's law," the concept does not apply at all to the country as a whole. Denmark considers most everything from its schools to its soccer team as the world's best, but is, at the same time, fearful of being overrun by larger nations, particularly Germany and America, in case these best things should be spoiled or even appropriated. Consequently, it is very suspicious of everything from a Big Mac, which is considered junk food, to the European Community, which is an attempt to take over Denmark's sovereignty.

America, on the other hand, being one of the most powerful countries, also thinks it has the world's best everything, in particular its way of life, and because Americans are so "benevolent," they wish the American way of life on everyone, believing that what is best for America is best for everyone else as well. America can't see that Denmark thinks it is doing quite well, thank you, without America's help; Denmark can't understand that America is only trying to be helpful and not necessarily trying to take over (even though that often does seem to be the result of American help).

Moving from one place to another—whether between towns, states or countries—always enables one to see things, both the old and the new, in a new light. I like to believe that I can give my students an insight into things American (when they feel like listening) that their Danish teachers can't and that I can maybe also interpret their Danish life for them in a different way, encouraging them to be critical of things that have always been done a certain way. Since I look at politics through my Danish-American eyes, I hope that I can also contribute new ideas where the old have become ineffectual. I am so much an American that I want to help where I see a need for improvement, although my own impact as a single person certainly cannot be so "dangerous" to the Danish way of life as that of my whole country.

DENMARK FOR BETTER OR WORSE

Dan Frickelton

At the time my wife and I decided to come to Denmark, I was twenty-seven years old and stood on the threshold of a promising academic career. I was very apprehensive about tearing our lives up by the roots, but certain pressures impinged upon our lives. My wife, a Dane, had been in the States for six years and was not altogether satisfied with her life. She was also pregnant with our first child and, for reasons I will never fully understand, decided that she had to go home to have that child. I was left with the strong impression that I could come along if I wished but that she was certainly going. Thus, the strong wish to share the experience of having a child, coupled with a modicum of adventurism, enabled me to overcome my misgivings.

The numbing shocks that were to alter our lives forever began rolling over us in bone-crunching waves a mere month after our arrival in Copenhagen during the summer of 1974. First of all, our son, for whose natural birth we had been preparing for months back in the States, refused to make his entrance in the natural way. He was taken by cesarean section under rather dramatic circumstances and damned near perished in the process. The trauma of this experience was, of course, offset by the fact that he was healthy, hardy, and normal. But I then found myself in the position of having to cope with buying diapers, baby clothes, buggy—in short, all the things we had thought we had plenty of time to choose together—in a big city in a foreign country whose language I hadn't even a passing acquaintance with. I learned a lot of Danish vocabulary in the process, and to this day, I don't know what certain baby articles are called in English.

It proved difficult to find cheap housing in Copenhagen, and we were getting on my in-laws' nerves. The solution was to move to Aarhus, on the mainland, where we found a tiny apartment in a student housing area. It proved equally difficult to find a teaching position, and I soon discovered that my American academic credentials were worthless. I was told rather bluntly that if I had any hopes of teaching at the university level I would have to secure myself a Danish education. The line forms at the rear. . . .

This was my first genuine crisis—and it made my mind reel. I was appalled by what I felt was academic arrogance of the first degree. The ensuing years would cause me to modify this judgment somewhat and to realize that Danes are merely smug, an affliction arising out of an otherwise justifiable pride in their system and way of life. At this point, however, I was angry, hurt, terrified, and faced with an awesome decision. I could return to the United States, presumably alone, and continue my life where it had left off, or I could become a homemaker/babysitter/student and begin from scratch at the university. To do the former would cost me my family, the latter several years of my life spent running over the same ground. It is said that Americans are possessed of an indomitable optimism. I would agree, and to this I would add a good measure of stubbornness.

I rolled up my sleeves and began sidling up to the idea of being a freshman again.

At this time, a few months after our arrival, my wife's world began to disintegrate. Many of the people she had missed so much during her six-year exile in the States and had dreamed of building relationships with, failed in various ways to live up to her expectations. Her cherished grandfather died; an uncle splattered himself all over a Danish highway; another dropped dead at the age of forty-seven; an aunt—the wife of the splattered uncle—collapsed as a result of the loss of her husband, suffered a stroke, and has been a total invalid ever since. (Hold on, folks, this is only the beginning.) Her father died unexpectedly at sixty-three. He had been her refuge in the storm. Cousins and old friends turned out to have lives, families, and friends of their own and not so much in common with her as she had thought. All of this happened within our first year in Denmark.

I was still plugging away at the university and, by now, had lined up some work teaching English to adult Danes at the Extension University. My wife was working full-time teaching Danish. We were working hard at our respective tasks, trying to deal with our respective sorrows and disappointments and to ignore the ugly events of the previous year. Somewhere along the line we also began to ignore one another.

Buy house, make baby, start afresh. An ancient formula that never succeeds. We separated in 1979, the four-year-old moving out with me, the baby remaining with his mother.

At this point, I was approaching the end of my studies and working full-time teaching translation at the university and Danish for foreigners. That meant that my studies had to be relegated to the back burner for a time. I had a heavy teaching load and a child to feed and clothe. Priorities.

Up to this point, I had done nothing in Denmark except cope with succeeding emergencies in an effort to eke out a dignified existence in my new home. Life was such a struggle! Or so it seemed. Even the climate was a barrier: long, dark winters and chilly, disappointing summers. The Danes I found boring, socially stunted, inaccessible. When my son and I moved into our new apartment, none of our new neighbors made an effort to welcome us, let alone lend us a hand with toting furniture and boxes of belongings. Old images of Welcome Wagon visits, once representative to me of America at its silliest, now made my breast swell with warmth and longing. I recalled how, during my childhood, new neighbors had prepared food for my family and helped with the moving on the three occasions when we had pulled up stakes. Undaunted, I decided that Muhammad would simply have to go to the mountain. I started knocking on doors and introducing myself. Only once was I invited in for coffee. For the most part, my brazen behavior clearly unsettled my hibernating neighbors. I learned that Danes don't appreciate unexpected guests dropping in. I was beginning to get homesick.

The first thing I had to do was sort out my new roles and situation. I was full-time father for one son and part-time for the other. I was used to parenting and housekeeping, so there were no difficulties in that department. Being a bachelor again was both exciting and unsettling, and not without complications. I discovered that apartment complexes, such as the one we were living in, were refuges for divorced people, most of whom were flailing about in a more or less desperate search for a new mate. I found it difficult to maintain ordinary friendships with these women. They wanted more. On the whole, it seems to me that Danish women are not good at living alone. So I broke some hearts during the course of the next five years, all the while busily licking my own wounds, taking stock of my life, and making adjustments in my behavior, values, and viewpoints. I cherished and nurtured the few true friends I had, displaced foreigners like myself, almost to the man. I gradually settled down and took comfort in the routines of daily life: work, shopping, housework, spending time with my kid(s), secure and comfortable in the knowledge that I could survive well—if not ideally—on my own. I didn't need a woman for the nesting functions that all too many men can't relinquish, and this realization was incredibly liberating. Sex was easy to come by, and I was learning to procure this while avoiding the unpleasant entanglements of women on the sense of humor, and helpfulness while despised by others for the same things, which they in turn perceive as brashness, shambling simplemindedness, giddiness, and a tendency to be intrusive and aggressive. Every time you hear Danes criticize your country or its citizens, you have to suppress the urge to leap blindly to the defense. You are always insecure and left wondering if this is the way they see you. You admire their historicity, their consciousness of being a very old nation and the continuity that this imparts to Danish culture. At times you despise the very same things, which you now perceive as ancient rot, stifling cultural uniformity, and mind-numbing social homogeneity. At times Denmark appears to be well-ordered, well-manicured, squeaky clean, and relatively free from social ills. At other times you feel that Danes are miserable, neurotic, and suicidal, moving through their days like zombies, their tight, synthetic smiles barely concealing their lack of enthusiasm for life. Sometimes the corduroy trousers and home-knit sweaters appear to be borrowed from Big Brother and worn as outward tribute to the boredom within. Yet others spend small fortunes on the latest fashions, the most tasteful architect-designed furnishings for their homes, and expensive German cars. These same people will never offer you a cigarette because they are so expensive and will offer to buy one from you if they're out. No Dane would ever dream of asking for a free cigarette. As insignificant as these things may seem, they are, nevertheless, representative of the woof and warp of life in Denmark. Danes are, by turns, envious of one another and smugly self-satisfied; noisily critical of practically all other nations and pathologically cautious themselves; hibernatory, territorial fanatics and compulsive club formers. In many respects they are mild-tempered, humanitarian people who, like the few very rich Americans I have ever known, tend to be obsessed with the notion that everyone else is a free-loader out to abuse their hard-won prosperity and security. Two expressions are constantly disturbing the airwaves wherever Danes are gathered: "Danmark er et lille land" (Denmark is a tiny land) and, "Jamen, har vi det ikke godt?" (Now I ask you, what more could one want?). Smallness, smugness, a sense of security and of well-being—key notions for a Dane.

America stands in contrast with its vastness, sense of endless space, violence, and dazzling change. America is anything but a cozy, secure place to hibernate. That, among other things, is what makes it such an exciting place to be. On the other hand, when America is not being exciting, it's just downright terrifying. You can starve to death in the richest country in the world; you can be assassinated for your political beliefs in the world's oldest democracy; you can achieve success beyond your wildest dreams in the land of milk and honey; and you can die of appendicitis in New York for want of the sixty dollars necessary to gain admission to an inner-city hospital. Danes don't understand any of this, and neither do I. It tends to make them even more smug about their system. It just makes me sad.

When Danes ask me if I intend to return to the United States one day, I usually answer that I would very much like to but that I would have to have something to return to. I have a family, friends, a good job, a home, and I need not fear the consequences of losing my job, becoming an invalid, or needing an expensive operation. The price for freedom from such anxieties is high—roughly half of what I earn. But like any Dane, I too believe it is well worth the price. I remarried last year and have had my life graced with a third son. My new wife is eager to try living in America, so the topic is very much alive in our home. She is a registered nurse and would have little difficulty finding a job in the States. My position is more uncertain, and I'm not willing to pull up stakes in Denmark to move back to the United States on a lick and a promise and run the risk of never finding an acceptable job. Meanwhile, I consider myself well-off in Denmark. One has, perhaps, a little less, but one enjoys it more. Being a foreign national, I am not permitted to vote in Danish national elections, but this is offset by the fact that I may participate in local elections.

I will never be a Dane and, for this reason, will probably never feel completely at home here. But I don't honestly know if I could ever feel completely at home in the States again. I would have to live somewhere not too distant from the sea where the liquor store stocks Danish beer and *snaps* (schnapps).

AMERICAN DANE

Brian Patrick McGuire

I came to Denmark in February 1971, after teaching at St. John's Liberal Arts College in Annapolis, Maryland, for six months. I quit my job there because I felt that my Danish wife, Ann, and I could never accept living in America. The school was too elitist. Many of the students were screwed up because of the status race or because of service in Vietnam. There were lots of drugs and nervous breakdowns, and at the same time, the teachers were organized into a kind of little Neoplatonic clique that espoused a terrible conservatism—they supported Nixon when he went into Cambodia in May 1970, four months before I arrived from Oxford, having completed my doctorate. I should have gone to California, but I actually wanted to get away from California (I grew up in the San Francisco Bay area). So I live in Denmark because I chose it in 1971 as the only country besides the United States where I could live. We considered Britain, and I applied for a fellowship at Cambridge but didn't get it, so we stayed put in Denmark, and I have never regretted that decision. In 1976 I became a Danish citizen. In 1978 I returned to the United States for the first time and found a new generation in my own family, a changed attitude to politics after Watergate and the end of Vietnam, and colleagues in my field of medieval history with whom I have more in common than I do with my Danish colleagues. My Danish peers gave me a rough time of it in 1972–75 until I got a full-time position at the Institute for Greek and Latin Medieval Philology. Since then I have been able to be myself, to make my own way in the university, and to not have to worry about acceptance.

Since 1978, I have returned to the States every second year, mostly to California and to Michigan, where there is an annual medieval conference. I really need this tanking up in terms of books, ideas, stimulating conversations, and the chance to give lectures, and since I am not on the job market in the United States, my colleagues there treat me well because they know I am not asking them for anything except a night's lodging, good talk, and a lecture honorarium. I do miss the excitement and mobility of American life, but I think the solidity and relative quietness of Danish society suit me better. I like the security of medical care, even though the welfare state is more an American myth about Denmark than a Danish reality—especially when one thinks on the one hand of the taxes we pay and on the other hand of how little we get for our children in kindergarten, for big bills at the dentist, for new glasses, or for other expenses that are a constant problem for us. (My wife does not work, and I just scrape by now on twelve thousand crowns a month [approximately thirteen hundred dollars] after taxes.)

I think Denmark is a better place to bring up children than the United States—I have an adopted Korean son who will be six in a few months, and I never worry about his safety. I walk around in Copenhagen at all hours of the day and night and never worry about getting mugged. I know there is more crime and violence today in Denmark than there was fifteen years ago, but the level is still low compared with that of the United States.

I suppose that I have traded mediocrity for the brilliance of the upper echelons of American cultural life, but I don't think I would have been able to stand the competitiveness and superficiality of the American way of life—and the impossibility of changing society because of its size and the money interests involved. Recently, my wife and I have become involved in helping refugees. Here our individual efforts have had some effect. In America, I can imagine that we would have belonged to some illegal sanctuary movement and that we would have ended up being prosecuted for our efforts. Here, I think it is still possible to work through the system in order to make it function legally and justly for all, even for foreigners, while in America, the problems are so much bigger that a single human being can change very little. Nevertheless, there is a terrible smugness and provincialism in Danish life that comes with being in a small country on the outskirts of Europe and with not having the international daily contacts that one has in New York or San Francisco. Yet, when I think of middle America, Denmark is much more or ironic. And gradually, the country begins to assume a complexity, a fullness, and an immediacy that can only be expressed in hundreds of peculiarities, so that the question becomes absurd. Denmark has become a complete world, a complex realm where the expatriate discriminates between many things, and so the question becomes the unanswerable equivalent of, What do you think of your life? Yet Danes keep asking the question for years, as though the person had only just arrived, while for the expatriate, the real question has become, If I go back, how will I like the United States?

Since, as often as not, the questioner merely wants to make conversation, the expatriate simply develops pat answers. I say that I am in Denmark because I had a chance to work here, because the job was better than any job I could get in the United States at that time, and because it is interesting to live in Europe. All the replies are true, but none is the truth. Worse, as one repeats these answers, they take on a rather dead quality of some liturgy for a foreign faith. The real question is not why has one come, but whether one will stay. What are the terms under which it is possible to live in an alien social world where, no matter how well one learns the language or studies the society, one will always bear the mark of the stranger? In Denmark, where there is far less geographical mobility than in the United States, this foreignness is further emphasized because Danes have friends for life, starting in their earliest years. Their families are far less scattered than American families, and the result- ing dense texture of social life makes it exceedingly hard to get inside. Here, one can have colleagues and professional associates who never invite their fellows home, for example. The image of Danish social life, for the foreigner, can easily be that of the empty weekend streets where no cars move, no people appear, and a profound silence reigns from Saturday afternoon until Monday morning. The foreigner has little access to the private, weekend world, but he or she must try to be self-sufficient until the next week begins. And every evening is a smaller version of the weekend.

The expatriate must, therefore, have some inner resource, some work, hobby, or passion that fills these hours, that makes them not a period of boredom, but an opportunity to read, to work. Eventually, the social circle will widen but far more slowly than in the United

States. Danes almost never introduce one friend to another; they do not seek to bring like-minded persons together. Each connection will have to be carefully made and developed separately.

The Danish context does change the relationship of a writer to his work, at least if the writer is doing historical work. I cannot think in quite the same way about American history as I did in the States. Now I view it from the outside, from an older context, and from a country with an extensive system of social welfare. Each of these changes makes a difference. Viewing the United States from outside its borders throws the borders themselves into question. The naturalness of boundaries is an artifice of every culture, particularly when there is not a sharp language change at the border. The shape of the United States begins to look accidental, even temporary, rather than fixed or given. This sense of possible flux appears all the stronger in the light of Danish history, since the area controlled by the Danes has fluctuated wildly over the past one thousand years, at one point including half of England, all of Sweden and Norway, parts of Germany, and the Baltic area of Russia and Poland. Denmark today stands at the front line of NATO, keeping one constantly aware of that larger set of boundaries that have recently been drawn between East and West, with East Germany but a hop across the water. And since Denmark is a rather uneasy NATO partner, refusing, for example, to have nuclear weapons inside the country, the East-West border itself looks less solid, and certainly less justifiable, than it does when living comfortably far away in the United States.

The age of the European societies, likewise, forces any historian to rethink the American experience. While the too often repeated Danish remark that the United States has no history exaggerates the point, certainly there is a vast difference between a society 350 years old, which has written records for every time period, and a society whose roots go back thousands of years, before the invention of writing, before Christianity, before the idea of history itself. These differences do not register in obvious ways, but they are a subtle kind of pressure on experience. The existence of a monarchy, of people with noble rank, of an established church, or of any number of other institutions strange to an American, here remain unquestioned, accepted parts of life. It is impossible to rouse a discussion on the topic of abolishing state support for the church or for the monarchy. In analogous ways, social life is far more settled and less experimental than it is in the United States, a fact made obvious by the dearth of ethnic restaurants, the formality and length of dinner parties, or the ritual quality of vacation times that are far more fixed than in the United States.

And yet, Danish society, in other ways, is radically advanced in comparison to the United States. It has a more extensive system of welfare services than virtually anywhere in the world outside Scandinavia, and the United Nations gives it a nearly perfect rating on its quality of life index. Here, no one will be denied medical care or ambulance service because they have no money. Here, the state sends people to clean the homes, wash the hair, and cook the food of the elderly, sick, or deeply depressed person. Here, all education is not only free, but all university students qualify for state scholarships, which, though not enough to meet all expenses, certainly make it possible for anyone to go to the university. There are social classes, but they are harder to see. There is some poverty, but its discovery is a public scandal. There are fifty murders committed each year in a population of five million, but this is decried and thought to be excessively high. Living in such a peaceful, comfortable world, I cannot see the United States as I used to. It becomes at once disorderly and romantic and violent. Its corporations look far more powerful and far more dangerous to individual liberty, and its class divisions look far less justifiable.

These contrasts between the two countries register in my work as an historian. In teaching, of course, I address Danes on the subject of the United States, which forces me constantly to rethink the history of the country in the search for essentials. Automatically, I am forced into a certain amount of comparative work. In my writing, the comparisons are not explicit. The subjects remain the same, but I see them differently. I do not write as a Dane would about the United States, but neither do I write like an American at home. I refer not to the possible erosion of my active vocabulary or the danger that my prose will fossilize, but rather to the subtle shifts in my perspective. Too often, American historians write as if the injustices and problems of the United States were larger and more difficult than those elsewhere. The Mc-

Carthy period, for example, which I condemn as much as anyone for its intolerance, looks far less important when set beside other violations of human liberties that have recurred all too often in Europe. Or, to take another example, the American women's movement seems less radical and less important in light of the worldwide movement toward more equality from a Scandinavian perspective. Living in Denmark mutes exaggerations, making the United States doubly complex, interesting, and even strange. With luck, the same redoubling of values will occur in my work.

Strangely, however, I cannot say that I have learned much about the United States through discussions with my students or fellow faculty. In part, this is because virtually no university professor in Denmark has made the United States a full-time specialty. Most teach both American history and English history, or some other combination. Put bluntly, those whom I have met who are worth talking to professionally could all be put in a taxicab. No one seems to read the current literature in my field, and none of my students has reached a point beyond that attained by graduates of good private colleges in the United States. I do not mean to reflect negatively on all of Danish higher education but only to note the lack of any serious effort to promote study of the United States in particular. Paradoxically, a nation with an extraordinarily high level of English proficiency and reasonably good library collections has, as of yet, failed to use these resources when compared to neighboring Norway or Germany. Both have strong professional associations that meet once a year to hear papers on American subjects. Denmark has no association and, hence, no meetings. To counteract this situation, in 1984 I organized an international conference with fourteen speakers, inviting the colleagues from the taxicab. In short, in this lack, as in everything else, the expatriate confronts an empty space that can become the source of development or the excuse for disaffiliation.

But no amount of patient effort can make for a final integration. The expatriate remains alone, caught in a space between worlds, more vulnerable to the occasional loneliness, illness, and losses in life than those comfortably enmeshed in their home place. The expatriate remains constantly tempted to seek an impossible submergence in the foreign culture or to give up and return to the sanctuary of an old, familiar world. But this choice does not remain the same over time—the longer away, the harder it becomes to return home to an ever-changing America, where friends constantly move to new jobs, new homes, new horizons. One remains in a precarious middle.

This ambiguous position between two cultures can become the basis of an international sensibility. I try to resist the easy classifications of America and of Denmark and instead try to understand each culture as a complex whole. What I think of either country cannot be easily summarized as a result, but I can say that ultimately one feels like an anthropologist in each place: neither inside nor outside, neither alienated from nor integrated into either world.

A SOPHOMORE

William M. Woods

Your country: love it or leave it. I'd heard that often while organizing against the war in Vietnam. But when I did depart for good, I didn't do it to turn my back on America. It had acquiesced to my being a conscientious objector, which was one of the many breaks I'd had. No, I'm in Denmark because I wish to pursue the great American tradition of being an immigrant.

What I believe powered many an American immigrant, especially the ones who tried to keep up with the frontier (and maybe even shed a tear when civilization finally spanned the continent), was the hope of a moratorium on social convention and a fresh start. That's why a real cowboy hero rides off into the sunset and, though I'm no cowboy, that's why I came to Denmark.

Now, Denmark is a miniscule country that's more thoroughly organized than the United States; my tax rates make Americans gape, and there's no real wilderness here. So where are the invigorating opportunities and the individualism, you may ask, since you have certainly heard about the impoverished masses who traversed the Atlantic towards America for just such reasons?

You will be disappointed if you are waiting for some bitter anti-American polemics on poverty in the United States and the beauty of free education and health care. Of course, I admit to cherishing the freedom the welfare state's guarantees give me to focus on other concerns without worry. On the other hand, America possesses a vitality and a drive that I often miss in Denmark, but being a foreigner here has always forced me to probe my own thinking and this has proved to be a sizable compensation.

Although I feel that I am floating along with the mainstream of Danish society, I know that I will never really be a Dane. My accent will probably never completely disappear (despite the earnest efforts of my children), and I'll still think American in a number of ways. This means that Danes expect me to be different, and since they tend to be quite tolerant, the provincial folks generally leave me to my own devices, and those who are inquisitive keep intriguing me.

When I first came here for my junior year, I'd already enrolled in ROTC, but when I returned to the United States for my senior year, I was a conscientious objector. The reason was my achievement of the rather conventional goals of just about every foreign exchange program: get out of your accustomed American environment and experience the challenge of other ways of thinking and living.

In 1965 Americans were still something of a curiosity here, and those eager to learn Danish were something more of a curiosity. So I was treated most graciously, but sooner or later, Vietnam came up. My Danish friends were amicably dumbfounded over American policy, and since our discussions were hardly antagonistic, I wound up being my own worst critic. The unremittingly congenial reasoning of these Danes who gave comfort and support to the enemy was probably a major factor in my decision to become a pacifist.

It was this mild-mannered approach to life that became a strong magnet once again when I'd finished two years in the Boston ghetto, experiencing a firebombing and numerous robberies. So Denmark gave me a fresh start twice: first, when I needed to take a stand on Vietnam, and then when I needed my psychological batteries recharged after two years of being drained of the relaxed trust that is the basis of decent human relations.

Today, I must admit that I see the problems of the sixties and seventies as more complex than I did then. Neither Danes nor Americans seem to have a patent on solutions and, ironically, I find myself today criticizing Danish friends for opinions similar to those that lured me to this country in the first place. The more the United States military scores against terrorists and drug traffickers, the more I cheer. In a way, I've come full circle back to where I was at the beginning of my junior year. But then, doesn't the word sophomore come from thinking you know enough to be wise?

WHAT IS HOME?

Janet Rønje

I am an American woman who has been living in Denmark for fifteen years. I was twenty-five when I came here. I had long hair, blue jeans, a backpack, forty dollars to my name, and two summer blouses. I had been traveling around for three months, and I decided on an impulse to settle down in Denmark. It was the coziness that got me: the down comforters; the intense, inviting smell of coffee made by a person, not by a machine; and the late autumn sun that cast long shadows that nearly made me dizzy trying to adjust to the latitude. When I canceled my return flight home—*Where is my home? Is it you, America, with your too many packaged lifestyles to choose from? If I came back to you, which one would be mine? Can you tell me?*—it was November. It was snowing. I remember walking up the steps of the main train station and out onto the streets of Copenhagen after saying good-bye to my best friend and traveling companion. It was a moment out of time as I stood perched before my new city, my new continent, my new world. I was afraid, yet expectant. I had only new experiences before me.

Denmark let me in. It wasn't in the Common Market in those days, and there weren't so many refugees. Danish homogeneity was intact, and that homogeneity fascinated me. One people, one culture, one history that stretched like a comet's tail far back into time, back to Harald Blue Tooth and Gorm the Old. The Danes own their history like they own the ancient dolmens that still stand in the farmers' fields.

My mother and father were angry, so angry they refused—*Where are you Mom and Dad? I have missed you, missed you more than words could ever tell. I have never known you, adult to adult. I have become a woman without your witness. Does it help to say that now, at last, I understand your pain?*—to send me more than the sparsest of my belongings. It was difficult to write to them. They did not want to hear about Denmark, my kidnapper, so what had I to say?

I threw myself into my new life. It seemed far superior to the old one. The right combination of European savoir faire and Scandinavian enlightened society on a backdrop of castles, seagulls, chimney sweeps, and flowers. The young people were serious, political, ideological. The young women were earnest in their efforts to become more like men and the young men were equally earnest in their efforts to become more like women. The politicians made laws and more laws to prove that wealth and wisdom could be divided and shared in a democracy so that everyone could be the same and equally happy.

I was afraid that the Danes would find me shallow, naive, unpolished. I worked hard to become one of them. I studied Danish and cried over the impossibility of pronouncing *rødgrød med fløde.* I stood my grounds at butchers and tried to order unrecognizable meats while a crowd of impatient customers told me with body language that they had a lot of shops to go to before closing time at half past five. I learned centimeter and centigrade, opera and art, the names and faces of Danish actors—*Where are you, America? A plane ticket away. A day's ride. So out of reach. Perhaps next year. I remember some things—summer things—the sound of a lawn mower and a baseball game on tv, crickets singing outside the screen door. I am forgetting you.*—and Parliament members. Danish life began to be daily life, and the awe and the wonder gradually dimmed.

I met my husband, and we got married and had a baby. The public health nurse visited me as they do all mothers of new babies, and she helped me, thank goodness, as my own mother was far away. I cooked and cleaned and shopped and went to the doctor's, which is free. Money was a problem. A car cost a fortune, and the taxes kept getting higher and the benefits fewer. Sometimes the laws seemed like a straitjacket. You couldn't move, not up or down nor right or left.

We had another child. That makes two beautiful, blond-haired, Danish-speaking children. We read a lot of Swedish children's books, because they make such good ones, and Hans Christian Andersen, of course, the best fairy-tale writer ever, and at night I—*Where are you Mickey Mouse? Where is Davy Crockett and Santa Claus? Did I bring any of you with me, or did you disappear with my childhood when my parents sold our house and moved to Texas? Will my children ever know you as I did?*—sing them lullabies in Danish. Their favorite is a hauntingly melancholy one that goes in part: "Why does it become night, mother, with its dark and bitter wind? Hear the little cat, mother, it's meowing to get in. The seagulls and terns have no place to live. . . ."

We live out in the country, at the far end of a little country village. There's a grocery and a bakery of sorts and a gas station. The rest is people. From the window in front of my desk, I can look out over a big field and I can't see any houses. I watch this field change all year long, from the cold, hard, broken earth of the long winter when Denmark is blanketed in darkness to the first wet sprouts of spring. On midsummer night's eve, I can look out over the field nearly all night long, it's so light outside, and they say that if you stay up long enough you can see the sun dance. You can nearly feel the earth turning up here, from equinox to equinox, and in the depths of summer, the land is one lush mystery of growth. The field has been harvested now, and soon the fog will hang low over the soil. Legend says that means the marsh wife is brewing her beer. I know this field well by now, and I know this land. It is beautiful.

So what is a home? Is it where you were born or where you live or something quite, quite else? People say it's where the heart is. Does that mean it's in my chest?

Contributors

Gregory Stephenson was born in 1947 and grew up in Colorado and Arizona State University and holds a Licentiate of Philosophy degree from Odense University. He has served in the United States Army Reserves and has spent a year in Vista. Having taught at Odense, Aalborg, and Aarhus universities, he now resides in Copenhagen where he edits *Pearl*, an English language literary review.

Barbara Brændgaard was born in Petersburg, Virginia, in 1943. In the United States, she lived in New Jersey, Ohio, Pennsylvania, Tennessee, and North Carolina, and was educated at Oberlin College, Colby College, and the University of North Carolina. She also has a degree from Aarhus University in Denmark. She lives in Rønne.

Dan Frickelton was born in Iron Mountain, Michigan, and has lived in Missouri, Wisconsin, and Minnesota in the United States. He was educated at the University of Wisconsin and at Aarhus University in Denmark. He teaches and writes in Hinnerup on Jutland.

Brian Patrick McGuire was born in Honolulu, Hawaii, in 1946. He was educated at the University of California at Berkeley and at Oxford University and also in Scotland and Vienna. He immigrated to Denmark after teaching at St. John's College in Annapolis. He lives in Copenhagen and teaches at the University of Copenhagen.

David E. Nye was born in Boston in 1946. He was educated at Amherst College and received a Ph.D. in American studies from the University of Minnesota. He has taught at Union College and at MIT and at Harvard University. The subjects of his books include Henry Ford, Thomas Edison, and General Electric, and his most recent research concerns the social implications of electrification in the United States. He currently lives in Odense and teaches at the University of Copenhagen.

William M. Woods lived in Pennsylvania and in Boston, where he served two years as a conscientious objector in Boston Children's Hospital. In Denmark he was educated at the University of Copenhagen and now teaches in a Danish gymnasium and owns a small computer products company. He lives in Bogense on the island of Fyn.

Janet Rønje is a writer who lives near Odense.

5

Living in the World

This chapter begins with a delightful, humorous essay by Linda Simonsen in which she reveals how she learned that Sacramento is not the center of the universe. The two succeeding essays by internationally recognized painter Clifford Wright and author Nathalie Melzer reveal perspectives of artists who clearly see the world with international eyes. Finally, painter and sculptor Rikk Towle discusses how living in Denmark, which means living in Europe, has taught him "the lesson of history" and contributed to the growth of his artwork.

AMERICANS LIVING IN DENMARK

Linda Simonsen

All depending upon the nature, degree, and variations of your psychological hang-ups (whether you are ready to admit them), living in Denmark can be best seen as a process with an ambiguous beginning that points in no particular direction. In my own case, I spent the first two years here stubbornly refusing to expel the strange glottal noises and indistinguishable gurgles that characterize the spoken Danish language. During that period, I was quite conscious of my superior worldly perceptions and cultural insights (something that is the birthright of every blue-blooded, steel-gutted western American child born and raised in the core of the fabulous state of California, which happens to be the most important state of the world's most dynamic and progressive nation). Most of my time was spent in carefully, indulgently trying to inform the ignorant natives that the universe revolves in endless echoing, ripplelike movements around Sacramento, California, which is the focus of all intelligence and endeavor. It took about two years to realize that nobody was really listening, that I would have to do it in Danish to make any lasting impression, and that my worldview might even need some adjusting to make room for at least one other center of importance: Tivoli in Copenhagen.

This painful revelation marked the second stage in my seven-year process of acclimatization to the little land of pork and butter. Circumstances forced me to at least make some attempt at the gurgles and gags that comprise the Danish vowel system, and I was soon eagerly making a fool of myself in earnest, but often, haphazard stabs at simple domestic phrases like, "When's dinner?" and "When's lunch?" A kindly farmer had taken me on to help with his cows and vegetable production, and after I had gotten the hang of saying, "Please pass the butter," I decided one day to venture further afield. We were all sitting down to a meal of bread and cheese after milking and I asked him, in Danish (almost), if he had a cream separator, as I had contemplated making butter out of all our lovely jersey milk. I have always been blessed with a lively imagination, and not knowing how to phrase "separator," I substituted "machine," the idea being to say—more or less—"a machine with which to deal with cream." Now, he was rather surprised when it came out, "Do you have an airplane?," and despite numerous repetitions, we did not come to any satisfying mutual understanding of the possibilities of butter making on his farm. So, I went upstairs to my room to paint and draw. Wishing to do a still life of some farmhouse crockery, I sent their youngest child down to ask for a pitcher that I could use. I had my paints out and was whistling in happy anticipation of a creative session with the children as audience to my brilliant artistic endeavors, art being, as they say, an international language without words—and what could be more appropriate? Downstairs, a raging, shrieking battle was ensuing that I assumed had nothing to do with me. The farmer's wife was evidently not very happy about something, and suddenly the oldest boy came in with a very red, contorted face and started saying, in broken English, that I was not allowed to paint his mother's pots or crocks or windows or walls or anything but that if I wanted to whitewash the stable walls, then that would be very nice. In hopes of pacifying the poor fellow, I frantically dug out my old sketches and paintings of farmhouse crockery to point out that, no, it was not the pitcher I was going to paint—rather, a glorification of it on paper. Needless to say, the woman was rather piqued and astonished at her son's next communication. She meekly handed over the controversial item for my painting, but she never managed to successfully hide her fear and distrust of the weird and often, in her eyes anyway, anarchistic, revolutionary, and eccentric habits of small American milkmaids.

REFLECTIONS
Clifford Wright

I came to Denmark late in 1956 because I wanted to see Elsa Gress. My other reason for coming to Scandinavia was that I am a Finn, born a Kallunki, but adopted by the Wrights in Cosmopolis, Washington.

Earlier I had come to New York from Washington to seek my artistic fortune after a sell-out show at the Seattle Art Museum. I got to New York via Chicago, where either Horace Caton or Langston Hughes told me to go to New York City instead. Once in New York, I met Leo Lerman, George Davis, and Iris Barry, who got me invited to Yaddo (the artist colony in New York) where I lived for nine and a half years. At Yaddo, I met Elsa Gress, who was a guest while I was working and painting there. She was a Flannery O'Connor kind of number pregnant with the child of Richard Warrington Lewis whom she had met in Leopoldskronen earlier in the season. After she left, I kept up a correspondence with her and heard about the birth of a bouncing, but premature, boy who became robust very soon and whose birth was paid for by the painting of a friend, Asger Jorn.

After a few years of sorting my life out, trying to find my father, whom I had never even heard of, and trying to face the horrible competitive world by leaving Yaddo, I arrived on a freighter at one of those ports in France famous for having been in the invasion (Dunkirk). My arrival in Copenhagen during the dark months never made any impression on me because Seattle and the Northwest, as I remember it, was much the same. The one thing I was disappointed about was that there wasn't more snow. As a child, I had thought there was never enough snow in Aberdeen, Hoquiam, Thechalis, and Seattle. Surely, here in the great Scandinavian north, there would be lots of snow. It was the only disappointment I ever suffered with Denmark.

Elsa, whom I married shortly after arriving in Denmark, was living in a small, primitive, but still cozy enough apartment on Teglgaardstræde in Copenhagen with her son David who was about four years old and very much in charge. Elsa used to make a very warming and invigorating drink with rum, lots of sugar, and egg yolks that we used to eat with spoons. One thing led to another, Denmark spread its comforts beautifully, and to this day I have never seen a place to rival it. Through all our vicissitudes, it has held up wonderfully.

Suddenly Elsa was pregnant again. I had shown my paintings very grandly at the Palais des Beaux Arts in Brussels, thanks to the efforts of a splendid Belgian poet and art critic Leon Kochnitzky. It was my usual kind of show with lots of praise in the papers and few sales, but it made me very happy. I came back to Denmark and, with a new child on the way, we started looking for another apartment. The child turned out to be a daughter named Barbara, who also was paid for with paintings, but this time by mine. We found a perfect apartment on Amagerbrogade with no bathtub, but an indoor toilet, a dining room, a bedroom, and a big space with sliding doors that could be a studio. The apartment also had a big bedroom for the kids and even a small room for Frøken Mørck, Elsa's old nurse, who was still able to totter around most efficiently but who before long could no longer mount the steps of the streetcars she had to take from our place to her home. Much to everyone's surprise, she took like a fish to water to the luxuries of the old folks' home she was offered and lived there to the end of her days. It was a life of luxury for her, she who had always slept on the floor, if anyone did, and took the leftovers from the table. Nearly ninety she got to be, and mad she was at the doctor who let her die of pneumonia at eighty-nine. We were able to sing her out of dying once—Elsa, David, Barbara, Jonathan, and I—but she only lasted one more day.

From Amagerbrogade, I was first able to appreciate the towers of Copenhagen. Right in the city you were conscious of them, but you don't at first look up that much. On Amagerbrogade, when we had American visitors, which was often, I would, after a big supper and a celebration in the Danish manner, take them the next morning down to Our Savior's Church. This church shows that the somewhat prosaic common sense of the Danes in everyday life is not the whole of it, for with its spiral gold and green steeple just behind Ved Volden, Our Savior's Church is certainly something out of the ordinary. Its seething stone angels, busily engaged in the free expression of every kind of personality, cling to each corner of the high-vaulted roof in all manner of violent attitudes. They sing gustily and play harps lustily, but they try to stay respectable, blowing long trumpets with an "I've never had a lesson in my life" attitude. And there are the cherubim with their huge fiddles and flutes and trumpets. There is no stained glass in this church; it is all spacious, light, and perfectly proportioned. I was a pallbearer for an American friend who was buried there (it was his neighborhood church) and the elongated, round-topped windows let in a subdued daylight that was more suitable to the angels' goings-on than any holy aureola, stained glass effects could have been. The organ loft is devoted to elephants and a whole forest of wooden foliage in gray. And the climb up to the tower along the outside golden balustrade was one of the efforts I now wonder how we could have enjoyed so much with the hangovers we must have had!

So, on to the fastest rising and falling jackknife bridge in all Europe that takes you by the stock exchange building with its tower of entwined dragons' tails. It is this building that Mariane Moore wrote a poem about on a postcard, as she confirmed to me on another postcard long ago.

But I skip around. Would I like to change anything about Danish society, interpersonal relations, politics, or temperament? The Danes make you feel as if you have never gotten anything out of your education. Talk ranges all around the world and back. Danes have not only read the newest American best-seller, but the newest English one, as well as the French and German ones.

As an author, playwright, and critic, Elsa had to give many lectures. When I first began to take her around to these lectures—after our second move to a perfect old schoolhouse, Aasø Skole, located in the exact geographical center of Zealand—I began to appreciate what Bishop Grundtvig (see chapter 1) had done with his folk high school program. Elsa took a batch of young actors and their young director, Tom O'Horgan, who was anything but famous at the time, around on her lectures to such wonderful places, and as driver and guest, I was enchanted by the hospitality, enthusiasm, imagination, and delight that the audiences—young and old—showed for what was presented. I thought then that artist involvement with the folk high schools was everywhere in Scandinavia, but I have since been told that only Denmark is so wise and that, even here, the activities are waning.

The tempo of the welfare state is leisurely; the medical care is exemplary; and socialized medicine seems to me to be a civilized behavior. The royal family takes its role seriously, and thanks to an intelligent young lady who is the queen and to her able and sophisticated husband, they live a productive and worthwhile life—both as monarchs and as artists and translators.

I am sixty-seven years old with grown bilingual children. Two of them have decided not to be Americans and the third, who lives in America, cannot be American, oddly enough, despite that fact that he has two American fathers.

And, oh yes, the one thing I would criticize the Danes for is their tendency to be too modest about their great country. And no,

I don't think of returning to the States, though I have no special complaints about it and did not leave for any specific reasons beyond the ones I've mentioned.

WARS FOR

Nathalie Melzer

In May 1975, I graduated from Bowdoin College with a B.A. in philosphy. There was hardly time to admire the diploma, for I was already en route to Denmark via Montreal. Two weeks later, on the thirty-first anniversary of D-Day, the Polish liner on which I was sailing arrived at Langelinie in Copenhagen. I was met by my husband, an American. Two summers earlier we'd worked with an international organization called World Federalists Youth, which in 1973 had its head office in Copenhagen. We became good friends with several Danish conscientious objectors who were doing alternative service at the "Woofy" office, and we were encouraged by them to move back to Denmark in 1975. Our reasons for wanting to live and work there in 1975 were still semipolitical—my husband had problems with his status as a conscientious objector, and in general, he felt strongly attracted to European, most especially to Danish, political traditions. Despite ties to France (I am a dual national), I felt ambivalent about immigrating to Denmark. But I was also more than eager to move away from the States for a few years at least. I knew I would miss my family, but after having lived in an eighteenth-century New England farmhouse for two years, the idea of moving back to southern California, where my family lived, seemed out of the question. Another motivation for heading across the Atlantic was our conviction that we'd never survive life in a big American city. European cities were far more tempting; Copenhagen would be an ideal blend of international and provincial living.

More than ten years have passed and at least as many major hurdles have been tackled and survived since then. I don't think it is an exaggeration to say that it took me at least half that time to adapt to Danish climate and temperament. It is more my own fault than anyone else's that I found myself quite isolated from people and things Danish until about 1980. In part, this was due to my work, teaching English at a private French school, a little bastion of *discipline scolaire*, an educational anachronism just around the corner from Copenhagen's red-light district.

But isolation was also due to the language of my host country. There's only so far one can come into the hearth and home of Danes until one has truly mastered the language, a deceptively difficult task, despite—or perhaps because of—the utter simplicity of Danish grammar. There are such subtleties, enigmas, and paradoxes about the life and language that take a constant effort to unravel, and still one cannot quite put a finger on what it is that keeps this little community of five million ticking.

There are just as many social and political elements that repel me in the States as attract me to Denmark now. If I had to name one key element that has enriched my life here, it would have be freedom. Denmark has offered me the kind of freedom I am convinced does not exist in the States, the freedom from fear, fear of fellow Americans one has never laid eyes on before and hopefully never will. For me, the physical freedom to move about alone without being constantly on guard for shadows concealing potential murderers, robbers, rapists, and thugs is an absolute necessity for inner harmony and creative activity.

Another aspect of freedom in Denmark that I admire is the sexual freedom. The attitude here towards human sexuality is much healthier than what I knew in the States where puritanism and promiscuity seemed joined in holy matrimony. Attitudes toward sex were so hypocritical, as I remember. Scandinavia is scorned for its liberal laws on pornography, but the market for hard porn is in the States. Snuff films are an American phenomenon. I grew up exposed to constant examples and looming threats of physical and sexual violence, whether in film or in life (the difference?), and an absolute minimum of "soft" eroticism. Much more aggression and sexual exploitation are tolerated in the States. In my youth, examples of simple love and compassion in human affairs were largely overshadowed by more (sexually) violent, sensational relations between people. I always knew "they"—the perpetrators of sexual violence—were "out there." The media, of course, was full of them. Violence sells well.

In Denmark sexuality is much more allied, I think, with human—male and female—emotions. Compassion for fellow human beings plays a far greater role in human relations; it is held up as a model in much the same way as "watching out for number one" gets successfully drilled into many Americans. This Danish phenomenon of compassion understandably creates some complications for aspiring millionaires, dictators, religious fanatics, racists, and sexists. Aspiring Picassos and Hemingways also suffer, of course. They will claim (especially many English-speaking ones I've met who just cannot understand what has kept the Danes grunting in potato jargon for these past thousand years) that they've become swallowed up in a parochial neighborhood whose gut reaction to artistic gladiators is "Slap af! Tag det rolig," a "Take it easy, have another Tuborg" approach to life that drives the self-proclaimed creative warrior even crazier than he or she already is. For how can you fight tooth and nail when the sidelines are full of well-meaning dentists and doctors ready to repair each cut and sore at a moment's notice? And not because it is morally right or good to do so or because they can make a mint, but simply because they have a talent; it must be used, not exploited.

I was raised by a compassionate, loving man. But, as a good red-blooded American, he took as his motto "All the power to them," referring to people who've worked their way from rags to riches, to hell with how. If only "All the power to them" didn't wind up expressing itself in big business and government, I wouldn't give it a second thought. But that little saying is so linked with a grotesque misuse of power—all of which passes under the label of American free enterprise, the American Way.

I also feel Denmark and Europe in general have a much healthier respect for foreign ways. This is not to say that Danes do not have affection for their own traditions and customs. They do. Nevertheless, they do not feel the necessity to ram their own traditions and customs down the throats of others. In fact, their respect for all human sexuality—their natural, healthy curiosity about the other sex in the early years of childhood—may account for their openness to other "aliens" in adult life. I'm not sure children get such a natural head start in the States.

Another aspect of Danish life that I enjoy is the humor—extremely subtle, just like the language. It takes years to catch on to, but the Danes have a certain reputation among their Nordic cousins for having inherited all the available silly genes in Scandinavia. It is the unsophisticated blend of a wise man's peaceful pipe smoking and ironic wisecracks that I have come to love about the Danes. As a writer and producer of plays, it is this kind of audience I feel I can address.

I've visited and talked to people in a dozen countries and found the human animal to be pretty much the same all over. But human potential and the freedom to express certain kinds of emotions seems more or less great, depending on the environment. I feel that kind of freedom is undervalued and stifled in the States, whereas it flourishes here. Despite my love and affection for countless individuals in the States, the American way of life, as a whole, poses as a negative model of how freedom can backfire on its citizens. The Danish lifestyle is a more positive model of what a responsible democracy can achieve. Perhaps the liberties a community wants to realize may simply boil down to a question of size and temperament. If my guess is right, then it is the smaller communities that keep the torches of freedom brightly lit. Were I living in the States, I would probably fire my creative endeavors with a raging fuel. Two visits back to America have persuaded me that I'd also be consumed in that fire. A more natural role for me is to find a community (or communities) I respect and fight to preserve them.

The quality of life that Danes have stubbornly fought to create is a source of constant inspiration for me. Were I still living in the States, I might find a small community of people to work with and fight for. But I'd never have peace of mind knowing that a huge chunk of my taxes fuels a military-industrial complex I have nothing in common with and do not respect.

There are as many good people, beautiful people, in America as there are in any community given the right chances. As a playwright, however, if there is anywhere that I can help a few individuals avoid the dangers that threatened me in my youth, it is here in Denmark. Unlike in the States, I feel people already have an ear tuned to the kind of language I speak here in Hans Christian Andersenland.

Living in Denmark, one is exposed to a fascinating social experiment. I have no doubt that the history and the results of this experiment will inspire many developing democracies. There are too many aspects of American free enterprise that I'd keep colliding into, that I've neither the strength of character nor imagination to wage wars against. I hope I can continue being privileged enough to keep refining my creative weaponry in the wars for, a life-style that has won my admiration and respect.

THE GHOST OF HISTORY

Rikk Towle

Living in Europe has given me the unique opportunity to learn a new language and culture as well as to examine my own American identity. I have spent nine years (over a quarter of my life) as a resident of Copenhagen, Denmark. Copenhagen is an attractive old city with green canals and verdigris spires. I've grown fond of this cool northern city with its salt air and sea-blue sky, its woolly gray winter days and the ecstatic light of the Scandinavian spring and the mild midsummer nights. During this period I have learned Danish and have become acquainted with a culture that spans several thousand years—from the little gold-plated horse and chariot buried in a bog by Bronze Age sun worshippers to the impassioned prose of Søren Kierkegaard's philosophical essays concerning people's relationship to God.

I have learned enormously from my experience living and working in Copenhagen. The Danes are hospitable and friendly, yet they
are also somewhat aloof with a tendency to keep the world at bay
with a mixture of irony and self-deprecating humor. They are prag-
matists who have a fine sense of design and a long tradition of
craftsmanship. They are tolerant, sometimes to the point of indifference, as long as the rights of others are not infringed upon. Danes
are more willing to compromise than to take an impassioned or an
inflexible stand on political or philosophical matters.

Yet, despite my attraction to many aspects of Danish culture
and society, I am always conscious of my own identity and culture
as an American born and educated in New England. Perhaps the
greatest value of living abroad is this double advantage of learning a
new culture while reaffirming one's own national identity.

The ghost of history has haunted me since my childhood. Growing up in Massachusetts, I was constantly aware of the rich history
of Puritan and Yankee New England no matter where I turned. Plym-
outh, Salem, Boston, Nantucket, Concord, and Lexington existed as
real places in my childhood, yet assumed almost mythic proportions
in my imagination due to their historic background. The past surrounded me and seemed as real as the present. At times it seemed
more vivid. Walking past the old Puritan graveyard in downtown
Boston—with its slate and granite tombstones inscribed with hol-
low-eyed death's heads and horn-blowing cherubs—the past seemed
as real to me as the noise of passing cars on Tremont Street.

I attended Bowdoin College in Maine where I studied art history. In the college library is a portrait of a young Bowdoin author
from the early nineteenth century. He is quite handsome with his
chestnut curls and dark piercing eyes, and he is dressed formally in
a collar and tie. The eyes of Nathaniel Hawthorne always seemed to
follow me as I left the library and crossed the campus past the old
chapel and the creaking trees on bitter January nights.

I traveled to Europe to pursue my study of painting and sculpture. After eight years' residence in Copenhagen I am still probing and
sifting through the layers of European culture like an archaeologist at
a dig. Living here has enabled me to study the great tradition of
European art at firsthand since I have been fortunate enough to visit

nearly all the major museums and collections on the continent. From my initial study of painting and sculpture, I have gone on to work as a sculptor—first in welded metal and later in terra-cotta and plaster. I am mostly interested in the problem of how to reintroduce the human figure as a motif in contemporary sculpture since its displacement throughout most of the twentieth century. Consciousness of the great tradition of Western figurative sculpture—from the Greeks and Etruscans through Michelangelo to Rodin to Henry Moore—has inspired me to work with the figure at a time when it is generally regarded as passé according to sculptural theory of the past twenty-five years.

My fascination with history is not merely nostalgia for some lost golden age, although I confess to feeling alienated in the plastic and technological times in which we live. A sense of history seems to me to be necessary to give meaning to the present. Without it, the bare facts of twentieth-century existence seem unbearable. One of the reasons I prefer living in Europe is the feeling of a living tradition that still permeates culture and society. This is quite different from the prevailing attitude in the United States (outside of New England and the South, that is) where so much emphasis is placed upon technology and science as if it were the new religion of our time. From Cape Canaveral to Silicon Valley, America is future-fixated and ahistorical, with little regard for social or cultural tradition.

There are, of course, positive aspects of this restless urge to experiment and innovate. Our most original literature, painting, and music springs from this same sort of iconoclastic, improvisational strain in which the American artist creates a totally new art form outside of the existing genre or tradition. One can see this tendency to "make it new" in such varied art forms as Melville's *Moby Dick* to Charlie Parker's jazz to Jackson Pollock's drip paintings. These are uniquely American art forms utterly unlike anything else in the western European tradition. Only a sensibility nurtured in the mobile, iconoclastic, experimental climate of the United States could have produced such works.

American art today seems to suffer from an overreliance on experiment and innovation. This often results in work that has a gimmicky, superficial quality. One has only to survey American

fiction, poetry, painting, and sculpture of the past twenty-five years
to see the lack of resonance and depth of feeling that largely prevails.
This is due, I believe, to a severed lifeline to history and tradition,
as well as to a fixation with originality and new technique. T. S.
Eliot's ideas about art and tradition are still as relevant today as when
he published his essay on "Tradition and the Individual Talent" in
1920. "Tradition," claims Eliot,

> cannot be inherited, and if you want it you must
> obtain it by great labour. It involves, in the first place,
> the historical sense, which we may call nearly indis-
> pensable to anyone who would continue to be a poet
> beyond his twenty-fifth year; and the historical sense
> involves a perception, not only of the pastness of the
> past, but of its presence; the historical sense compels
> a man to write not merely with his own generation
> in his bones, but with a feeling that the whole of the
> literature of Europe from Homer and within it the
> whole of the literature of his own country has a
> simultaneous existence and composes a simulta-
> neous order. This historical sense, which is a sense
> of the timeless as well as of the temporal and of the
> timeless and of the temporal together, is what makes
> a writer traditional. And it is at the same time what
> makes a writer most acutely conscious of his place
> in time, of his own contemporaneity.

I see Europe with American eyes. I see America with American
eyes that have seen Europe for eight years. Living abroad changes
one's vision. It enlarges one's native view and gives a new perspective
on one's own country. Europe seen with American eyes is both living
history and the relics and ruins of Western civilization from the
Acropolis to Notre Dame to the Berlin Wall. America is a young
culture with enormous resources and potential. We have an energy
and an exuberance, an innocence and an optimism that can inspire
the Europeans. Through their long history, which has witnessed the
rise and fall of many different cultures, the Europeans have earned a
bitter wisdom and a tragic view of life. We can learn the lesson of
history from them.

Contributors

Linda Simonsen, born in San Diego, California, is twenty-six years old. She attended school in Sussex, England, hitchhiked through Europe, married a Danish farmer, and worked in agriculture for five years before starting a degree course at Aarhus University. She has a son four years old and lives in Højbjerg in Jutland, where the people have a "down-to-earth way of looking at things humorously and, very ironically, preferable to Americans who take themselves far too seriously both linguistically and philosophically."

Clifford Wright was born in 1919. He has written books and exhibited his paintings in all parts of the United States and Europe. His paintings have inspired work by many poets and composers including Theodore Roethke, May Swenson, Ben Webster, Tom O'Horgan, and John Cage. He and his wife, Elsa Gress, are cofounders of Decenter "a sort of shifting and moving, but continuous, colony or commune" that is devoted to "keeping connecting lines working across the Atlantic." They are "convinced of the desirability, indeed the necessity, of the exchange of ideas and inspiration between artists of different nationalities and genres."

Nathalie Melzer has studied philosophy and languages at universities in New England, France, and Denmark. She has lived in Copenhagen, Denmark, since 1975, where her most recent work, a Danish-English musical entitled "Freya Lever," has received critical acclaim.

Rikk Towle was born in Boston in 1953. He attended Bowdoin College and the University of Copenhagen. With Welsh poet John Barnie he is editor and publisher of Razorback Press. He lives and works as a poet and sculptor in Copenhagen with Danish poet Karen Kolmos.

6

A New Home in Denmark

*Most of the writers in this book do not plan
to return to the United States. Nevertheless,
several of the following essays reveal that the
authors are still in limbo and that their feelings
about living in Denmark are still ambivalent.
In spite of this, these authors and those who
stay without reservations, have chosen Denmark as their home for a variety of reasons—
emotional, political, intellectual, and artistic.*

PIGS, WEEDS, AND DOGS

Julia McGrew

Expatriation and exile, imposed from within or from without,
and emigration are the quintessential experiences of the last few
centuries. The three words summarize the vast shifts of population
from rural to industrial areas, from Europe and Asia to North and
South America, from the United States back to Europe, principally
to Paris, and more recently, from less industrialized lands to western
Europe. They remind us also of the movement of writers and artists
from the West Indies and India to England and America, out of Nazi
Germany and Soviet territories to Europe and America. Cultural
shock and a deep fracture of language and traditions has dominated

much of human experience since the late fifteenth century. I am no historian and therefore will not try to fill out this large, bold, introductory sentence with statistics and details. As a philologist, however, I want to comment on the terms *exile, expatriate,* and *emigrant.* Each word has its Latin forbear; each forbear has an already complex set of connotations almost inseparable from the literal meaning. An exile is one who is forced to leave home, banished, for one reason or another. He or she begins life in a new country unwillingly, unprepared, and without anticipation of happiness. From Ovid to Thomas Mann, from the self-exile of James Joyce to the enforced expulsion of contemporary Czechoslovakian and Chinese writers, the exiled artist wrenches new meanings, and new literary structures from the collision of different languages and different literary traditions.

The connotations of *expatriate* include dislike for and even condemnation of one's native land, and the hope of greater freedom, usually artistic and literary, in another country. Americans in Paris in the twenties are the most familiar group and have largely fixed the associations of the word. But Joyce in Trieste, Nabokov in Switzerland, and young Americans in Sweden and Canada during the war in Vietnam broaden the examples without weakening the central connotation—one who left his or her own country in philosophical and cultural disenchantment.

An emigrant is one who moves from one country to another—perhaps across an ocean or a continent—usually in the hope of finding a better life in the new country. Whatever the economic compulsions behind this move, the emigrant has some freedom of choice. (*Les emigres* after the French Revolution are in a special class, not the same as Irish immigrants to North America in the nineteenth century or Pakistani workers to northwest Europe in this century.)

To none of these groups do I belong. Simply, I retired from teaching at a residential college to living alone on a farm with pigs, weeds, and dogs as my daily preoccupations. The farm is in Denmark, not in the United States (where I was born, where I spent part of my childhood and all of my student years, and where I taught for almost thirty years) and not in Canada (where I spent the other part of my childhood and some of my adult years), because I fell in love with the island of Fyn when I lived here for six months in 1971. One can no more explain falling in love with a countryside than one can explain falling in love with a person—no rational or objective descriptions quite convey to others the exhiliration and the peacefulness of the state of living. Accept and enjoy with sympathy is the most one can say to others.

Essentially, I moved from cities to the country, from the thickly social life of a residential college to the largely solitary life of a retired, unmarried woman who must learn gardening as well as new traditions of daily living. Moles and mice are at work outside and inside my home. Chickens, geese, cows, pigs, and birds make the noises I hear constantly. I do not miss the racketing noise of cities or the grime and rubbish. I suppose I just prefer the different noises and kinds of grit in the countryside. I still miss students and colleagues—I miss that world painfully sometimes—for a lifetime of one sort of continuous exchange of ideas came to an end. But it was bound to do so at retirement, and better to put geographical as well as social distance between one's middle and later years. I enjoy struggling to live with a language that I didn't begin to learn until I was fifty-three years old (not that I shall ever achieve a native's accent or range) largely because English reveals its particular richness, subtlety, and humor in ways I had ceased to notice. (I had better say American English, for it is American idioms that I find myself constantly chuckling over or vainly trying to render into Danish. And the best dictionaries of English-Danish are primarily British English, with little, if anything, of American colloquialism or idiom.) Who can translate the comment, "He's way out in left field," without giving a detailed description of baseball? Who can observe of an automobile that "they haven't ironed the bugs out of this one yet" without subjecting a Dane to the history of garment workers in New York City in the last century? Equally, what does one mean by *pretty* in English? The Danish variants (*smuk, køn, pæn,* and more) seem easily distinct from one another to a Dane. If I say "smuk," the echoing agreement is, she is indeed "pæn." And so it goes. I like the violence of slaying down the grass instead of merely mowing it, and I am enchanted to butter my bread and also to have my automobile buttered at regular intervals.

Out in the Fynsk countryside where I live, the rain is wetter, the icy wind more biting, the birds more melodious and various, the air far cleaner than where I lived the past twenty-five years. That's not to say that the world here is better than the one I left, but I do find it far, far better. Teaching in a small college consumes all one's time and nearly all one's imaginative energy. At least that's what it was like for me. Here, I have all the time in which to read, to write or to fail to write, to make a good garden or to fail to make a good garden. Hostile judgments and intrusive friendliness are alike unknown here, just as affectionate criticism and friendly concern are always at hand. Certainly, I must seem peculiar if not bizarre to my neighbors: whoever heard of an American who does not own and will not have a television? Whoever heard of a retired professor who carpeted and lined the walls of a farmhouse with books (never high enough to obscure the windows, of course) and then began to raise dogs? Puppies gnawing on the *Oxford English Dictionary*, adolescent dogs devouring Shakespeare in paperback, moles pocking the whole lawn, mildew etching and blotching Henry James and Faulkner, (but not marking, mysteriously, Dickens or Johannes V. Jensen), and water voles rearranging my tulip and daffodil bulbs so that every spring these flowers bloom in unexpected and disordered places—all these curious problems delineate my world here, but they do not offer ground for any social or cultural judgment.

I have not yet succeeded as a gardener much better than I have in speaking Danish, but I am still working at it. When I first moved here, I scarcely knew a petunia from a peony. Ragweed and roses I knew for both make me sneeze violently, but vinca I thought a nasty weed and the first sprouts of carrots were, I thought, a new kind of fern. I live in a farmhouse, in a traditional Danish arrangement of a *gaard*. The house faces one side of the courtyard, the other three sides are enclosed by farm buildings. One of these buildings now houses an antique reaper and an almost antique Ferguson tractor; the second houses a fascinating collection of old pipes, hot water tanks, half a horse carriage, a high-seated bicycle, beams, tarpaulins, ropes, broken lanterns, and rusted bedsprings—just the sorts of things one might need at any time on a farm. The third building did have stalls for cows and goats but is now a large, airy indoor doghouse

from the puffin burrows (and against human commands), and they can stretch their front legs out at right angles to their chests. This enables them to go head first into a burrow and retrieve a puffin without alarming the birds by scrabbling and digging their way in. It also enables them to become flat as a plate and escape under any sort of gate or hedge. They are a little taller than an American cocker spaniel or a Corgi, but they have short, flat fur. Their ears are furry, pointed; their noses, pointed; their tails, bushy. They do resemble a fox, for they are beige and reddish brown with darker single hairs over their shoulders, and they have white markings on their chest, legs, paws, and the tip of the tail. They are thoroughly intelligent, sociable, comical, and energetic. They apparently do not feel themselves exiles or expatriates in Denmark, where we now have fifty-four of them flourishing, although we can offer no puffins to hunt.

I moved to Denmark with the intention and hope of becoming a Danish citizen, but this takes time. I don't think in terms of better or worse in politics or in the quality of everyday life. And although it is true that we have a better system of health insurance and hospital and medical care here, we pay for it. The same evils I perceive here, I long perceived in the United States. I did not flee them in moving to Denmark, and I am not now criticizing Denmark for them. They are those forces and directions of this century that I deplore, work against, and will continue to work against as long as I live. These evils are the encroachment of commercial standards on scholarly decisions and in academies of the humanities. Here, as everywhere, television and all other mechanical reproductions of life move like juggernauts through cities and villages, crushing individual imagination and individuality in language and fantasy, numbing both the power of memory and the possibility of concentration.

So here I am, old, old-fashioned, and immeasurably happy in a fairly undramatic landscape that boasts neither mountains nor fjords but that subtly draws the eye over amber reeds and blue-green algae to the farthest line of birch trees beyond the shallow inlet. The small fishing villages around the coast of Fyn are daring even in stormy weather in their red houses, blue or orange front doors, varnished and painted boats in white with red or brown decks. The innumerable manor houses inland on Fyn have preserved the old relationships of

woods to tilled fields, of lawns and hedges to the manor house set
back against beech, birch, copper beech, and chestnut trees. There is
less unworked land here than in the United States. Indeed, there is
less of everything, and of what there is, it is almost always smaller—
an automobile, a park, a foot or hand, an income. Perhaps that is
why it satisfies me so deeply—I can see it and grasp the relationships
and the patterns. That's how I know I am at home.

TO MAKE SOME RETURN

Terry Culler

Why do I live in Denmark? Why do I not live in the United
States? It's been years since I really thought about why. My leaving
America was accidental, not ideological. I've always loved America,
and although I once said I'd leave the country if George Wallace were
elected President, he never was and I probably never would have left
for that reason. But one vulnerable summer in Ireland, I met and fell
for a Dane. By the time (one and a half years later) we decided to live
together, I had finished my M.A. and had moved to a new place with
my three-year-old son. Thus, I'd already pulled up stakes, moved
away from my family, and was feeling very much at loose ends. My
Danish fiancé was only in the middle of his studies in Aarhus, so
Denmark won by default and we moved here.

But why did I stay, even after the breakup of that first partner-
ship? The obvious reasons are the personal connections: my little
half-Danish son, of course, and his father's family, even though the
man himself had, shall we say, lost his appeal. I was also falling in
love with another Dane but could have persuaded him to try
America. Now I'm a willing member of his family, and we have two
small children. Easy reasons, but maybe not the deepest. I guess I
simply put down roots for the first time in a life filled with move-

ment. I had to make clear to myself what I was doing and where I should do it. I could see I'd be doing the same in America, but likely feeling more anxious.

So of course I've thought about returning. It would be unnatural not to. I'm an American and have never seriously considered changing my citizenship. But Denmark (or Europe) and I get along very well. I love to visit America for a month or two, then come home to Europe. Denmark and Europe feel like home.

There's plenty I miss about America besides the special Americans who help me keep the post office in business, especially my father with his understated humor. I miss the wonderful landscapes, especially Arizona's mountains and deserts (or what can be seen of them through all the new housing developments and shopping centers). Denmark's cozy, but you don't come for the scenery, climate, or food. I also miss free access to things like tennis courts—they require club membership here—vegetables out of season, cheap restaurants, and the widespread lively arts (although I finally saw the New York City Ballet in Copenhagen). There's simply more of everything in America and I miss it.

If I left Denmark I would surely miss the nearness to the rest of Europe and the languages I play with every day. I'd miss the peace and country style I've grown used to here, Copenhagen, and my mother-in-law. I like drinking tea in the afternoon and getting around more on my bicycle than in a car. I also like the remnants of an older social structure, now that it's no longer binding.

My Danish is good enough to get me into whatever I want, but English remains my home language. Sometimes it's more "Danglish" because you get lazy when both languages become second nature, but I doubt I could live with a Dane who hadn't mastered English. Before I understood Danish as language and only heard the sound, it sounded so ridiculous that I'm sure I had a mental block against learning it. It took me two years and a move to the country to get my act together. Many Danes are helpful but are simply not used to hearing Danish spoken by foreigners, so getting understood at first is a real exercise in aggravation. The reward comes later because Danish is an exciting language to use and write. It can still be hard for people who aren't used to my accent to decide if I am making wordplay or if I should be corrected, but at least I'm enjoying myself.

I would love to make Danes less complacent, and I'm sure 99 percent of the foreigners here would second that. If you want to bring up a Dane's latent nationalism, just insult Danish food (which I do rather often). My own little anecdote about Danish complacency comes from Odense University, where I was hired to teach American literature. I couldn't get the program accepted for credit towards a degree even though I had several semesters behind me from Arizona. I appealed and the university's review board nearly laughed the English Department out of the room. Their decision held until I'd completed my semester's teaching. The English Department was actually represented by a resident American professor, but the attitude is thoroughly Danish. Danes' opinion of their sublime educational system (and equally sublime Christmas pudding) ranks right up there with their opinion of God. But then, Danes are seldom spiritual beings. They're often mentally lazy and apt to distance themselves ironically from anything requiring too much thought. If Danish institutions and media seldom act rashly, it's probably because they've debated the issue to death and missed the deadline.

Back in the States, I'd love to cut down the noise—to allow a few hours in the day without television and advertising and stop pushing the American Dream from every corner. I really fear the violence in America now and the seeming acceptance of it as just one more fact of life. If Danes debate every subject to death, Americans too often start swinging with no talk or thought behind their actions. And American competitiveness turns every success into a question of beating or bettering someone else. One American friend of mine who was an exchange student in Denmark twenty years ago liked being able to play the violin here without being judged a fairy. I think this kind of attitude is changing in America now, but the cowboy myth is likely to be around for a long time.

On the positive side, though, is the enormous energy in America and the acting on convictions. Scandinavian social welfare (very praiseworthy) can lead to laziness: "Let the government handle it." Americans know that the government won't handle it, so they'd better do something to help each other out of bad conditions, and they do. There are many good and tolerant traditions when anyone bothers to think about them. But the best thing about America is Americans: friendly, curious, good at having fun and improvising. Danes could use a shot of that flexibility.

In the seventies Danish universities were full of Marxist students who showed solidarity with the working class by sporting overalls that would never see elbow grease and who spouted a jargon that would bring the strongest worker to his knees with laughter. I knew several who traveled off to America with stern faces to confront the monster of capitalism on its home ground. They came back and began saving up for their next trip because—surprise, surprise— they liked Americans. (To their credit, they admitted it to both themselves and other comrades.) Ditto the Swiss stewardess who got a tad weary of being patted on the bottom and called sweetie pie, but who appreciated the American who forced a smile when she doused him with coffee at the bottom of an air pocket. A Frenchperson or a German would have wanted her fired. My mother-in-law guides tourists around Copenhagen and gets to know many of them since she speaks seven languages. She gets tired of Americans' constant need to stick something in their mouths, causing them to disappear at stops that weren't intended for foraging. But she agrees they're fun and seldom blasé, even when the crown jewels don't really interest them.

I like Danes, too. Both Danes and Americans have the virtues of their vices, and that must be why my likes and dislikes sometimes sound contradictory, even to me, and I'm trying to say what I really feel! Danes require more getting to know. They're not as openly friendly as Americans, but then they're usually free of the superficiality too much cheer can have. They certainly respond to open, friendly types with the awareness that there might be something to learn from them. My own two Danish families' warmth and acceptance of my son and me have certainly helped us feel at home. The aristocrats are more boisterous, raised as they are with the idea that anything goes as long as it goes in style, but my first in-laws were quiet, staid West Jutlanders. I always felt like a rogue elephant crashing into Bambi's forest when we visited, but they always perked up and made me welcome. We must have been good for each other because I'm less noisy now and it's an improvement. The ironic distance that can be maddening when it blocks understanding becomes delightful when it turns inward, and Danes are very good at laughing at themselves.

I like the eleven- or twelve-party parliament, where most every political direction really is represented, and I like the relative peace of Danish society. There's violence here, too, and it's increasing (where isn't it?), but Denmark has shown itself capable of learning from other countries' experiences and works to prevent as well as to punish crime. I don't see any tendency here to start packing a rod. I'll even have to get a weapon permit to bring my late husband's ceremonial sword back from America. I find it a reasonable request. I like the way groups get along, too, the way school sociability is for everyone, not just the superpopular in pairs. And if Danes are inflexible as regarding the use of a degree in anything but a narrow field, they do have a school course of study for about anything you'd want to be. It's recognized that everybody's good at something, even if the emphasis, both here and in the United States, is on academics with an eye toward future business and money, money, money.

I've gotten used to a more relaxed way of looking at many things here. I'll never forget a topless swim from a deserted beach near my parents' home in Oregon five years ago. I'm usually too shy to go topless, even here where it's old hat, but my son Mike and I were strolling along the beach in Oregon when we discovered that we were all alone and the water was too inviting to pass up. We waded out in our underwear and were happily sloshing when we spotted a lone man with a cocker spaniel on a leash, obviously enjoying the view. I modestly turned my back and waited for him to go away. When he showed no signs of budging, Mike sang out in clear prepubescent tones, "Hey, Terry, I think that man likes you!" That got him moving so fast his dog could barely keep up, and Mike and I moved on home, howling all the way. When I told my parents, I expected we'd laugh some more, but my mother was furious. All of her aggravation with the society that had swallowed up her daughter boiled over. I was not in Denmark anymore! That libertine behavior didn't go here! Why couldn't Danes ever keep their clothes on and think of something besides sex? That man could have had me arrested, and it would have served me right! What had Danes ever accomplished, anyway? And so forth. I suppose I could get used to the stereotyping and the super-America attitude again, but it would not be easy.

Yet, it's hard to compare the quality of my life in the two countries. The violent headaches that I battled in the United States are gone here, and I've learned the value of a quiet thought instead of constant action. I thank the low-geared Danish society. I live in the country but am close to the city. This is possible in a small country, and it means that city and country aren't at odds with each other, that people with backgrounds like mine get along fine with the farm families and are not hounded by gossip or suspicion, as I'd feared. I don't miss living in a city, but I would miss having one nearby. That's no problem here, but it might be in the United States. I also have an unusually inspiring and just plain fun marriage here, but there are good men in America and I might have found all this in the United States had I been there for the last twelve years. In a free society if you have a reasonable income, the quality of your life is still mostly what you make it.

I've tried teaching, writing, and sewing for fun and profit both here and in the United States. Denmark enhances my creativity in one way: it encourages me. There's not yet any tradition of using up and throwing away. I sew children's clothes from old clothes and anything else I can get my hands on, mostly for the fun of it and to help the family income, but I have been able to earn money both sewing and showing others how. My mother sends the kids beautiful clothes from America, but there's a Care Bear, Donald Duck, or Ohio State insignia on every single thing. Cute perhaps, but impersonal and unoriginal. Here, recycling is in among more than just the aging flower children. The small size of the country and notice paid to someone who's considered an interesting foreigner make it easier to make contacts and, for example, to get articles published, which encourages me to go on. But there are clearly more impulses and excitement in America.

I definitely contribute more to Danish society than to American society because I've matured here. I left America at twenty-five and hadn't done much more than to get my education and mother my fatherless child. In Denmark I've taught both adults and children, led a children's club, and chaired the local school board. I've also written some terribly earnest articles about women's changing role and its effect on children. (I've translated the best one and sent it off to the United States.) In America I wrote two children's books that were never published and some sensitive teenage articles for the daily rag when I was in high school. There wasn't much more. I hope to do some more writing and working with women and children as I get more time and energy because it's very important to me. If I could make my mark as a humorist on both sides of the Atlantic, I'd be jubilant because I can't keep from judging myself by American standards. But it doesn't really matter where you contribute as long as you do. People's needs are the same all over. Little lovely Denmark meets my needs, and I want to give something in return. I guess that's why the roots went down at last.

MY LIFE IS HERE

Margot Gunzenhauser

I first came to Denmark in 1970 on foreign study. After graduating from college in 1971, I got a job in Copenhagen and came back. I didn't know whether I would wind up staying for six months, a couple of years, or the rest of my life. In the fifteen years I've been living here, I've often been asked whether I came here because I was in love with a Dane. The answer is that I wasn't in love with any one Dane, but I did like the Danes as a group. I liked their relaxed tempo of life, their humor, their language, and the fact that Copenhagen functioned more like the small midwestern city where I went to college than like the metropolitan area near where I grew up.

A lot has changed in the last fifteen years. Vandalism, violence, and crime have steadily increased. More of the distrust that people feel for strangers in big American cities is now felt in Copenhagen, too. It upsets me that the Danes have been unable to see societal problems coming and do something to attack their causes, instead of waiting to see the same effects as in the United States, Germany, and other more stressful countries. Back then we had a picture of Scandinavians as being somehow more enlightened than the rest of us sociologically—probably because of the welfare state concept. Now times are worse economically, some of the welfare state's principles are being eroded, and we are seeing that the Danes do not have the magic key anymore than anyone else does. The influence of American culture, especially popular culture, is very strong here. But fortunately we are still lagging some years behind the United States in various measures of societal decay.

When I moved here in 1971 I made no special efforts to contact other Americans living in Denmark, although I did meet a few by chance. I already spoke the language and knew a good deal about the day-to-day functioning of Danish life, and I was more interested in associating with Danes than with other expatriates. Around 1979 I started playing more American folk music again. I had played in the States, and my instruments were some of the first possessions I brought over here, but through the years I had almost stopped playing because I had no contact with anyone else who did. That changed when I got acquainted with some Danes who were interested in old-time and bluegrass music, including the man I eventually married. An association was started for old-time and bluegrass, and I became active on the steering committee and also edited our magazine for three years.

Around the same time, I became interested in calling square and contra dances. I started teaching adult education classes in 1981. I had previously been very active in international folk dancing and had taught it at college and a little bit here. With the square and contra dancing, I found a niche that was waiting to be exploited and that became my specialty. Now, five years later, I'm beginning to get a reputation around the country. I have been on national radio and even television, and I'm writing a book in Danish about American folk dancing.

It is a little strange that I have become so heavily associated with American folk culture, since I am not the type of American who clings to her nationality like a life preserver. I think I was able to do this and feel comfortable about it because I first had acculturated myself to my adopted country. I will never be 100 percent Danish—just having an accent is enough to preclude that— but on the other hand, I'm certainly not 100 percent American any- more, either. Although I've been fortunate to be able to visit the States an average of once a year since I moved here, I still find myself gradually growing away from American society and finding more and more things there that seem unfamiliar or undesirable. For the most part, these are small, everyday things. I've never been too involved in politics, either here or there. There are also small, every- day things that I miss from the States, of course. The huge variety of different foods, for instance, although that is one area where Den- mark has been catching up. There is much more available here now, both in the supermarket and in restaurants, than there was when I moved here.

Most Americans who live in Denmark feel the smallness of the country. With only five million people, everything is more inti- mate—everyone watches the same television station, hears the same radio broadcasts, and to a great extent even reads the same newspa- pers—and there are only a handful of people at the top of any profes- sion, public or private. This can get a little claustrophobic, but it can also be positive. It binds us together. Even now, with everyone talk- ing about stress, life here is much less hectic and more predictable than in New York, for example. Competition is less fierce, but on the other hand, excellence is more rarely achieved. It's a two-sided coin.

My husband and I have sometimes talked about going to live in the States for a year or two, mostly so that he could improve his English and have a chance to experience more of American life than he can in a few weeks' vacation. He has a number of interests that draw him to the United States, and I, of course, have my family. We probably won't wind up moving, but even if we did, I have little doubt that it would be a temporary move. When people ask whether I intend to stay here and whether I miss the United States, about the only thing I can say is that moving to Copenhagen was not that much different than moving to Chicago or Atlanta might have been. My life is here now—my work, my friends, my habits—and unless some specific reason comes for me to leave, I expect to stay.

THE LOVE IS INEFFABLE

Kenneth Thomas Tindall

I live in Denmark because Denmark has been my home since 1960 and I am happy here. I do not live in the United States because the long exile beginning in 1957 has turned out to be permanent. I left the United States with the equipment of a pioneer, in the personal and moral sense, at the age of twenty, and made a life for myself here. I had various personal and political reasons for leaving the United States. One of the former is that I wanted to write. One of the latter is that I received a medical discharge from the United States Navy and was subsequently unable to obtain work in that country except by dissimulation. Most of the things I think I miss about the United States no longer exist except as treasured memories, such as Estes Kefauver in a coonskin cap riding in a convertible down Fulton Street in Fresno, California. Fulton Street no longer exists. I know that I would miss just about everything about Denmark if I returned to the United States to live, for this is where I am at home and where my love is and where I am now nearly fifty years old. I know that I would miss my young Danish wife terribly. I do not wonder what living in the United States would be like and never consider taking up residence there again. Should I return sometime for a visit, it will not be before I have three novels in print in the United States. I think that there should be drinking water in the Danish trains and that equal child custody rights should be available to divorced and single fathers. In my opinion, the United States would benefit from socialistic political solutions. Besides being a beautiful country, the United States is endowed with the potential for solving many of the problems that have beset humanity, such as hunger. Denmark and the Scandinavian countries as a whole have, in spite of limited economic and physical resources, largely succeeded in eliminating their social problems, while at the same time providing their citizens with the greatest possible personal freedom. In the United States an individual must be comparatively wealthy in order to secure a quality of life equivalent to that enjoyed by the vast majority of people in the Scandinavian countries. Living in Denmark, I seldom hear or speak English, and I think this fact enhances the quality of my writing. My ear is better able to distinguish between the gold and the dross in English, and it fleshes the language out, so to speak, with a palpability and plasticity inconceivable in a situation of unrelieved immersion in an English-language advertising and entertainment culture. Besides, whatever my own writings have contributed to Danish society and culture, I think that I contribute to the promulgation of Danish society and culture abroad through my translations of Danish texts. I have translated very many of the scripts of the most distinguished Danish films of recent years. I have also translated Bodil Kaalund's *The Art of Greenland*, which was published by the University of California Press in connection with the Scandinavia Today cultural exhbition that traveled in the States a couple of years ago. And I have translated Carl Nielsen's *Fynsk Foraar (Springtime on Funen)*, which Norman Luboff performed with my translation in North America. Hopefully, these translations are a contribution to American society and culture as well. My novels, too, it is hoped, with their quality of social analysis, may impinge in a positive way on the American psyche. I regard these activities as being of the greatest importance.

I went back to the United States in early 1968. One of the reasons I went back was because I had seen pictures in Danish newspapers of tanks in the streets of American cities. One typical trait of the Danes and the other Scandinavian nations, I think, is a natural eagerness to be of aid to other human beings instead of, for example, constantly and as a matter of principle, finding opportunities to exploit them. I shall never forget the loving kindness of my Danish friends, many of whom had problems connected with drugs, in giving me a place to live and food and love when I got back to Denmark in 1969, skinny, mute, and afraid. Again I went back to the United States. I suppose I wanted to see it from its best side and not its worst.

In 1971 I was working in the shipping and receiving departments of a factory in Long Island City. One day I picked up a keg of screws from a pallet, and the keg came apart in my arms. A long splinter from a broken stave jabbed deep into my left arm and I was sent to the company physician, who had his office in a building on nearby Queens Plaza. He extracted the piece of wood, cleansed the wound, and gave me a tetanus shot. Now this doctor was an old Italian American named Pasquale Paciantine; he was easy to talk with and he had a natural gift of healing. And so for a couple of years, even across the city, I would go to him for various small ailments, such as a case of ringworm. He was an old guy, closer to seventy than sixty, and he was getting ready to close his practice. I remember the equipment in his consultation rooms was old and primitive, antediluvian, like his autoclave, and it made me think of the thrift that was a necessary virtue of the immigrant people in making a life for themselves in the New World. His diploma from the Cornell University Medical School was in a frame on the wall along with his New York State license to practice medicine. I thought he looked like Arturo Toscanini. (When I was six somebody gave me an album of Brahm's First Symphony with Arturo Toscanini and the NBC Symphony Orchestra.) Dr. Paciantine was one of your old-time general practitioners, and he was a very cultivated person. He had seen a lot of life and had known a lot of different kinds of people. I liked to talk with him about what I was doing, that I was involved in writing a novel about America and Americans. I remember that in one of our conversations—he had been talking about his retirement—he summed up his experiences by saying that the United States was no longer a civilized country.

Living in New York City was an adventure, and I suppose you could say I had a good time there—a lot of women (including experiences of exquisite delight), a lot of drinking in good company, and a lot of humorous experiences. I managed to get a better-paying job with the United States Postal Service and one of the places where I worked was a vast, single-story structure covering many acres in Queens. It had formerly been the film studios of the United States Army Signal Corps. After the war it had been made over into the military postal concentration center for the East Coast in combination with the Long Island Postal Terminal. Thousands of people were employed there, and many of the postal workers were middle-aged guys, overweight and alcoholic, real Charles Bukowski type postal stiffs who walked with a "slob land slouch." The fact is that all of them had broken arches: their feet had been destroyed by years of pushing canvas tubs full of parcel post across an infinity of concrete floors. When I started working there, I wore a pair of leather work boots that were like combat boots. They had been all right for walking on a hickory-block factory floor, but after an eight-hour tour on the floors of that post office, I was so tired I could hardly walk to the subway station. So one weekend I wrote home to Denmark to my beloved former second wife, Janne, and asked her to send me a pair of clogs. She sent them from Copenhagen by airmail, defraying the postage difference herself. Well, the reaction of those old postal workers was really remarkable. They had never seen anything like Danish clogs—wooden shoes with low leather uppers you simply slip your foot into—and can there be anything more un-American? I remember one middle-aged white guy asking me what they were like to walk in, and I told him they were like walking on water.

As I mentioned earlier, I couldn't get a job after I had gotten out of the Navy with a medical discharge. Years later, I encountered the same fear among the postal workers in the United States. They were afraid of the street, of being fired from the postal service for some infraction, and thus being severed from employment in the public sector or in those areas of the private sector where there is security and an opportunity for advancement. What this amounts to is that people are afraid of being set out on the street to beg for alms. I find this truly barbaric. In other words, the American concentration camp is the street. This omnipresent fear, like a clenched fist over the head of the individual, not only inhibits dissension, it also automatically contributes to the proliferation of the criminal class and other self-given rise to the unbroken folklore of love that is part of the American cultural heritage, too, like a gift of God. I have many fond memories of the United States, but as I say, most of those things no longer exist, like Mrs. Crockett's scrod and playing cowboy pool with Mr. Crockett at the MacDowell Colony. Sometimes, though, something makes me feel homesick, a few bars from Dvorak's New World Symphony or an Indian word. The words *Allegheny* and *Mononga-hela* are enough to give me goose bumps, as well as an old green memory of hitchhiking in rural Ohio, the twilight like burnished copper and a C & O H-8 class 2-6-6-6 hauling a mile of coal. But these memories do not make me want to return to the United States, for the United States is not like that. More than ever, I think, the United States is a culture of allure, an allure adhering to a certain transience—nay, nomadism—of American life that is an effective temptation, perhaps especially for kids. There are still young Danes who have a hankering to go to the States, get hold of a short and open 'er up on the long straightaways and, like, disappear. But they know better and instead become Danish world champion dirt track motor-cycle racers. I haven't owned a car since I was sixteen in Fresno, California, and that is the only time I have had a driver's license. I don't watch television, either—don't even own a television set. I had good, concrete reasons for leaving the States, and I have never regretted it. My attitude to being an American living in Denmark can be summed up in the homily, "I couldn't be a good Dane if I weren't a good American." I may never return at all. We are creatures of free will, and the God who gave us life gave us liberty at the same time. And if ever the allure of America gets to me and makes me feel like going back, I have only to look around me and think of the epiphany of strolling with my wife in Folkets Park in Malmø, Swe-den, on a hot summer day and hearing the band play "Amazing Grace."

I think that being an American writer living in a non-English-speaking society makes it possible for me to renew the language on my own terms, uninfluenced by the osmotic stress of the popular culture.

I have never had to dissimulate in order to get a job in this country. I have never been dismissed from employment here, nor

Contributors

Julia McGrew is Professor Emerita of Vassar College. A distinguished medievalist, author of studies on Chaucer, and translator of Icelandic sagas, she is currently Visiting Research Fellow in the Centre for the Study of Vernacular Literature in the Middle Ages at Odense University. She lives in Kertinge on the island of Fyn.

Terry Culler was born in 1946 in Salt Lake City and has lived in Washington, D.C., Colorado, Arizona, and Ireland. She has an M.A. in English from the University of Arizona and a minor in history from the University of Odense in Denmark. She lives, writes, and sews in Søllinge on the island of Fyn.

Margot Gunzenhauser was born in New York in 1949 and grew up on Long Island. She graduated from Earlham College in Richmond, Indiana, and has studied at the University of Copenhagen. She currently lives in Lyngby, near Copenhagen, where she plays her music, teaches dance, and works as a writer, editor, and an illustrator.

Kenneth Thomas Tindall was born in 1937 in Los Angeles. He has also lived in New York, New Jersey, Ireland, and Paris. His novel *Great Heads* was published by Grove Press. *The Banks of the Sea*, a novel that chronicles the return of an ex-Vietnam Navy veteran to New York City after expatriation in Europe, will be published by the Dalkey Archive Press.

7

Impressions: Creativity, Comparing the Two Cultures, Limbo, Living in the World, and a New Home in Denmark

The following quotations are excerpted out of context from original submissions that could not be included in their entirety. They may not, therefore, adequately reflect the author's original tenor and tone. For example, from a generally positive essay about the United States or Denmark I may have excerpted a negative message (and vice versa) because it shed additional light on the issues discussed in the essays that were used in their entirety.

CREATIVITY

I do not know if my creativity is enhanced by living in Denmark, but because of my music, I have met many inspiring people and found adjustment to life here much easier. . . . Many of my friends here on the island [of Bornholm] and in Copenhagen are musicians, and because of my active music life, I no longer miss contact with musicians from my years of study in the States. —Hattie Andersen, musician

I received my undergraduate degree in music and although I never pursued music as a profession, it was a cherished avocation for as long as I lived in the United States. In addition to teaching privately in my home, I was also a member of two different orchestras; I played various professional jobs on a free-lance basis and studied with the principal flutist of one of the country's major symphony orchestras. I came to Denmark with high hopes of comparable musical involvement. But I was disappointed. Finances didn't allow for private lessons with the principal flutist of the symphony orchestra in Odense, which ultimtely preempted my chances for professional musical involvement. In my investigation of the various amateur orchestras in Odense, I discovered that the quality of performance to which I was accustomed in the United States, was sorely lacking in Denmark. Eventually I became discouraged and more or less gave up on the possibility of establishing a satisfactory musical career. —Heidi Knudsen, musician

In my experience as a musician and teacher working with older music (mainly Renaissance and some baroque), I expect that there is more readiness to understand the inner calm demanded—and conferred—by this music in northern Europe than might be the case in the fast-living States. . . . Although there is no way of knowing how things would have developed had I stayed in America, I feel that exposure to European culture and to Danish taste and living has enhanced my appreciation of the quality in both the fabricated and the natural environment. —Oliver Hirsh, musician

Professionally, Denmark is a good place for me since my field is animal behavior, especially the field of acoustics. Denmark is very strong in acoustics. Also there's as much, if not more, research going on in Europe in the area of my interest than in the United States. —Lee Miller, teacher/scientist

It's easier to get unemployment benefits in Denmark than in the United States. If people are unemployed and know how to use their time, they can then explore their creativity to produce or do whatever they wish with their lives. In that way, their creativity can be increased. —Daphne Lynn, teacher/visual artist

Yiddishkeit in Denmark

this is the land where—as the story goes—the king
   himself
put on the yellow star
and from which fishing boats sped dark-eyed
   families to safety
in Swedish harbors:
       we have friends here
but as for yiddishkeit
you have to make your own
so I propose a kit containing the following
   provisions
for nostalgic refugees from Flatbush:
one suntanned grandpa looking good in red striped
   pants
and telling jokes;
one clarinet solo from any Jewish wedding;
one yahrzeit candle;
one mother in orbit around her child;
one constellation of aunts and uncles on a porch
   on a summer evening;
one hot pastrami sandwich on club;
one schlemiel, one schlemazel, one schmeggeggi.
           —Richard Raskin, writer

COMPARING THE TWO CULTURES

It is not surprising that a 1985 book, *Danish Quality Living* by Ed Thomasson, has intrigued me. If we measure quality of living in terms of material goods, our standard of living is much lower in

Denmark than in the United States. We no longer have a large home, two cars—or even one—a large washing machine, dryer, dishwasher or various smaller electrical appliances. If, however, we measure quality in terms of our environment—such as healthy bike riding daily, neat and clean streets and countryside, and clean air—it has improved.

The move to Denmark has forced me to review what is important in my life, what gives my life its quality. Seeing friends often, which is possible when most are less than a twenty-five-minute bike ride away, means more to me now. I take more time to write friends and family in the United States. John (my husband) and I spend more time together, for he is on the road to work only ten minutes on a bicycle path. Life is simpler. —Caroline Olson, writer

I am a pacifist. As such, I detest the Soviet Union and the United States for perpetuating a state of seeming emergency so that it appears necessary to the people of both countries to maintain an enormous military establishment such that the armaments business has become the single largest industry worldwide. The military-industrial complex (as Eisenhower termed it in his farewell speech years ago) has established a condition of instability especially in Europe, which assures its primacy in the economic and political thinking not only within these two countries but also within the NATO and Warsaw Pact countries. Even so-called neutral countries like Sweden depend upon arms production in order to fuel their economies. I would like to see Denmark pull out of NATO, but its minimal participation does not irk me that much. By and large, this is a peace-loving country and I like that. —Ben Livingston, teacher/chemist

There is much too much television in the United States. Denmark's one station is rarely on more than eight hours per day. The fact that most of American television is so exceedingly lousy is just grease on the fire. I was back in the United States for two months in 1985, and much of the television programming I saw turned my stomach. The regular news programs are tragic farces, proclaiming objectivity and professionalism while handing out slop. Several shows I saw I took as personal insults. I think it's a plausible theory that Americans get too much of their reality from television nonreality—not to mention their political opinions. I think it is a sickness, and it's very sad. —Mark Kline, musician

I think it's easier to be a white American in Denmark than a black American in Denmark. Some Danes seem to be prejudiced against blacks. Some Danish musicians were surprised that I, a white, was working with and hanging out with black musicians. They didn't believe that existed in the United States. A Danish musician asked me once when a black musician and myself were together, "Are you guys really friends?" —Robert Rockwell, musician

I believe, with the Danes, that education should be free through college and professional school for all who qualify and that no one should be denied health care because they can't pay for it. It is a humane society and one which prizes order, unspoiled nature, democracy, and relaxation. Who would willingly give up these qualities in exchange for the violence, filth, inadequate medical care, homelessness, traffic congestion, and anticommunist witch hunting of the United States? —Caroline Olson, writer

I feel very free and have always felt free to tackle jobs in the way I preferred. I suppose the American in me says (when Danes are afraid to try something different), "Let's give it a try. If it doesn't work, we'll do it another way." —Lydia Zachariassen, musician

Danish society seems a little stiffer than American society. Entertainment in the United States is often not as structured as it is here. When my sister has a party in California, there are people from all walks of life. Here people tend to cultivate smaller circles of friends, depending on their work or their education. My American friends seem a little more casual and easygoing than my Danish friends. They also enjoy laughing a lot and have a good sense of humor. On the other hand, the longer I live on Bornholm, the more I feel attracted to the special mentality of the islanders. If they pay you a compliment, they really mean it. Their vocabulary contains fewer superlatives than the usual American vocabulary. When an islander says something is *halvgodt* (half-good), he means that it is excellent. —Hattie Andersen, musician/teacher

Generally, I think children here become more aware of their desire and need for independence and find respect from the older generations. There are many juvenile lost souls both here and in America, but self-respect and self-reliance come earlier to kids here. Several of our American visitors have commented on what a good environment for children Denmark seems to offer. Distances are closer, traffic is less awesome, and exposure to violence and media rape is minimal in comparison. —Meg Larrabee Sønderlund, writer/artist

The place where I work full-time—an advertising bureau—happens to be quite a pleasant environment, mostly because of the people I associate with. They're open, caring, and intensely loyal companions, without that sort of hardened edge that I think characterizes many in American business.

Nonetheless, working in business—especially as a woman—is not easy here. Businessmen are accustomed to taking only other men seriously. But I'm perservering, joining all the right male-dominated clubs and writing in *Borsen* (a business magazine, which has a predominately male readership) in hopes of establishing my credentials and convincing them I'm good at what I do. —Valerie Navarro, writer/businesswoman

There seems to me to be two paramount differences between the United States and Denmark. To begin with, people in Denmark are taught from an early age that the selfish pursuit of one's own self-interests sometimes has to be subordinated to pursuit of society's best interests. I find it sad that Danes can use the United States as an example of the unfortunate things that can happen when people ignore the best interests of their society.

The other major difference is that in Denmark no judgment is made about those on the bottom, no matter how they arrived at their condition—whether, for example, by birth or apathy. Generally, Danes believe it is in the best interest of their society to actively seek reintegration of the "loser" into the mainstream of society. —Ray Miller, teacher

LIMBO

A few years ago I dreamed nearly every night that I was flying back and forth from here to the United States and that I was really confused about where I ought to be. Now I feel more at home in Denmark than I did before, thanks especially to my teaching and minimal mastery of the language. I also know, however, that deep inside I'm an American and I plan to return to the United States in a couple of years. I will always love Denmark—it's my home also—but I do feel the need to integrate America in me and vice versa. I will regret having to deal with certain things in the United States, though: pollution, crime, paranoia, ideas like Star Wars, and blind national loyalty that disregards the need for world solutions and understanding. —Daphne Lynn, teacher/visual artist

I have to admit that living here in Denmark I've found it easier to become part of the society. In the United States I felt completely isolated from mainstream America from the time I was eighteen years old. On the other hand, I'm not a Dane either. I think as a jazz musician, you are a jazz musician—that is your life. You're an artist, and an artist is an observer, and an observer is by definition an outsider. It might even be dangerous for the artist to lose the observer status—the distance. —Robert Rockwell, musician

I often have guilt feelings about living in Denmark because of my American family. The Hintons have kept quite a detailed account of their family history. We seem to have been among the earliest founders and settlers of America—fought for the right side in the Revolutionary War, the wrong side in the Civil War. My father's father was the first white boy born in the Oregon Territory (so we claim). . . . It happens that I am the only male Hinton to have a son and he lives in Denmark. I feel that I am a bit of a traitor by living in Denmark because the Hinton name in Washington State will be gone. I am sometimes asked by Danes if I will become a Danish citizen, and why not? I can only answer that I am an American, I feel American, my family history is American. I love America. —Doug Hinton, entrepreneur

On 9 March 1984, I started the United States Women's Club of Fyn for American women living on this island. . . . The club has certainly been an advantage to my living in Odense. I feel more relaxed and communicate with such ease. I don't have to worry about where I should place the adverb while I'm speaking. Furthermore, we can laugh at some of the crazy constructions we make or words we have forgotten in English because of the Danish influence. —Patricia Johnson, teacher

LIVING IN THE WORLD

I wish I could say that my creativity has been enhanced by living here, but I am not sure it has been. My adaptability has been, of course, and that makes me a better individual, I think, because I am more open to other ways. —Ben Livingston, teacher/chemist

I will never consider myself Danish, nor even be accepted 100 percent by Danes. On the other hand, I'll never be 100 percent American. Americans, on the whole, are very isolated. Having lived in Europe and traveled widely, I've lost my innocence. Things like NATO, EEC, World War II, and European history are no longer mysterious or romantic terms. That's a big advantage to living in Europe. —Ed Kowalski, writer

Since my husband and I have many friends and acquaintances in many other countries, we don't have much patience with this streak of Danish provincialism that asserts that Danes are somehow better than others and that we don't really need the rest of the world. (But Americans often have that irritating trait as well.) —Lydia Zachariassen, musician

When leaving New York twenty-three years ago, I set out for adventure and a chance to practice and develop my talent as an artist. My family and I regard our frequent visits to the States with the same expectation and excitement as our visits to London, Paris, Rome, and Lisbon. The adventure continues. —Ronald Burns, painter

I would feel totally unnatural if I did not speak American English with my children, teach them the songs, and read them the books I knew as a child. And of course I feel it natural, as a parent, to tell them of the places and people I have known. They know my whole network of family and friends in America, and we are all eager to check the mailbox every morning. Their Danish father informs them of the Danish facts and fictions of his life. They will become more shaped into Danes by their Danish schooling, which will include a wider perspective of the world as a whole than I was exposed to, but through me, they will maintain a natural sort of American identity, and I hope they will be able to have some of their later education in America. I do not want them to grow up to reject either country. I hope through our experiences as a family, with the people we know here and in America, we can act sort of as ambassadors—represent

both countries and help cultural awareness on both sides. —Meg
Larrabee Sønderlund, writer/artist

A NEW HOME IN DENMARK

We travel to the United States about every two years. The last time
we were there for two months, and we were ready to come home
after three weeks. But we stuck it our for two months, visiting friends
and relatives in all parts of the United States. When we returned to
Denmark, I remember driving down the road to our house. Normally
when you arrive home after you've been gone, you've got to wait for
your soul or your spirit to catch up with you, but when we turned
into the driveway, we felt as if our souls were standing in the door
waving at us, saying, "Hey. Welcome home!" —Pete Hunner, glassworker

8

Afterword:
A Dane in America

Peter Vinten-Johansen

In contrast to the other contributors to this volume, I am a Dane living in the United States, and I had little choice about leaving one country for another. Reversing the direction of immigration and eliminating the issue of choice provides an evaluative perspective on the contributors' remarks that may help clarify points of comparison, illuminate motives, and suggest the outlines of the expatriate syndrome in this particular group. But then it is only fair that I provide, as the other contributors do, the personal background underlying my point of view.

I came to the United States because my father believed that he could provide a better life for his family here than he could in Denmark. He had come alone to the United States in 1950 on a one-year fellowship to serve a residency in several hospitals in the Washington, D.C. area. I remember as a six-year-old in Denmark receiving frequent packages with T-shirts and toys that seemed to come from paradise. Postwar deficiencies in material goods and food were still a fact of life for most Danes, and we were no exception. The receipt of a crushed bag of potato chips had assured my benign compliance with my father's suggestion on his return to Denmark that we move to the United States at the first opportunity. But the costs were prohibitive at the time, and my father was obligated to give at least a year's service in Odense in repayment for his fellowship. I don't remember much discussion of a move thereafter, although I was then preoccupied with my first year of school.

Then came my first decisive contact with the role of chance in human affairs—my parents won a Volkswagen bug in a raffle. There was none of the ballyhoo often associated with such an occasion, however. The hospital was pushing its employees to sell tickets, and my father hawked his obligatory batch among the merchants in the neighborhoods outside the hospital compound where we lived. When he ended up with seven of them unsold when it came time to turn in the raffle stubs, he bought the remainder himself and promptly forgot about it. The winning stub was drawn at the gala dance, but no claimant appeared until my father found his stubs several days later while changing his pants. He was the winner. Suddenly he had an automobile in Denmark at a time when the old poster of Danes on bicycles who stop traffic to let some ducks cross the road was still within the realm of the possible. He owned a car, but he couldn't afford to drive it very often. It was usually parked in an alley nearby, covered with a tarpaulin to keep tree sap and organic bugs off our mechanized "bug." One afternoon when I was at school, someone who could afford to drive a car in postwar Denmark offered to buy it and returned that night with more cash than I had ever seen in my life. There it was, stacked on the living room table in a bunch of piles for all three kids to gawk at. It suddenly became clear to me why it was there for us to see: we were going to the United States!

We crossed the Atlantic in February 1952, on board the passenger ship *Stockholm*, before it became infamous for its collision with the *Andrea Doria*. Few people today have any idea what it means to be in the Atlantic at any time, let alone in February. Those who have had this experience will understand why this eight-year-old maintained a seven-day lip-lock on our stateroom toilet. I remember little else after the first morning in the Skagerak as my parents pointed out the distant Norwegian shoreline. I was, however, transfixed on the double order of eggs, sunny-side up, that I had requested before I realized why the table service was placed on wet napkins. I eliminated the sight of the eggs by vomiting on them, then found myself hustled to the stateroom and put in a bunk. Several days later (a calm day, I was told), I stumbled to the deck for some snapshots that barely suggest the deception some parents are willing to undertake to send photographs to the folks back home. My greenish hue wasn't captured on black-and-white film, but mountainous whitecaps provide ample evidence that this was no pleasure cruise. I made it to the railing when some passengers disembarked at Halifax, but then it was back into the bowels of the ship for another night of dry heaves. I stayed with the ballast when the rest of the family rushed to the port side to view the Statue of Liberty. Even the sidewalks of New York were undulating for several hours after we landed, although my first sight of black people within an overwhelming mass of humanity gave me something to think about other than my queasy stomach. Only then did it begin to dawn on me that I—not the blacks—was the freak on this side of the Atlantic. But America was land, if nothing else, and at that moment I would have chosen to be a landlubbing freak rather than endure another ocean voyage back to what was familiar—or what I thought was familiar, for the endless days and nights in a tossing ship was like a rite of passage that had already obliterated much of my own past.

There came many hours in the next few months, however, when I would gladly have exchanged my daily life for an endless February in the Atlantic. The gradual, ineluctable destruction of my native language undercut whatever sense of self-confidence I then had about my ability to understand the world about me. The change was not without its salutary effects on my personality, although I didn't realize it then. At eight years of age, I was already very left-brained in thinking and behavior—primarily verbal, logical, and cerebral. It didn't take me long to realize that I could communicate more effectively in second grade through gestures, facial expressions, drawing, and nonverbal sounds than with my precociously overdeveloped Danish language. My home provided little reprieve from painful hours in school. My father, who insisted that we become inconspicuous ingredients in the American melting pot, did not permit us to speak Danish in the house. He was rarely home during those first few years as he worked in three different hospitals, but the sight of his Oldsmobile 88 at the curb set me in fear and trembling of the English quizzes that awaited me when I entered our half of a duplex in Alexandria, Virginia. He would point to ceiling, floor, wall, door, window, and various objects and furniture—all in rapid-fire order—and woe to me if I didn't know the English word for each. There was no physical punishment, but he knew that I knew that his disappointment in my halting efforts was sufficient for me to stop speaking Danish even when he wasn't around. I still remember lying in bed at night, testing myself for the next quiz and consciously erasing Danish words from my mind. As I write this, I am forty-three years old and once again comfortable and fluent in Danish; yet I still find myself in situations where I must struggle to find the simplest Danish words—inevitably, they are words I worked extra hard to repress so that I could please my father by speaking much like every other kid in our neighborhood. Those were times when many immigrants to the United States did what they could to hide their ethnic distinctiveness.

Exchanging my language, my knickers, and my long hair for English, blue jeans, and a flattop were the next stages in making me feel like a real American. I soon adjusted to American life, made new friends, and overcame the painful experiences that every immigrant has in a new land. In fact, I used several extended visits by my grandparents to make another break with Denmark and to congratulate myself on my good fortune at having been extricated from their inflexible adherence to provincial mores. Leaving home for college broke more ties with the past, especially the daily contact with Scandinavian furnishings and decor that my mother had refused to relinquish. And when I decided to leave medical school to become a historian, I really believed that, in breaking the Danish tradition of the oldest son following in the footsteps of paterfamilias, I had emerged as a complete American at last.

To this day, I'm unsure whether internal or external factors first caused me to reevaluate my American self-image. Although I had often felt that I was different from my friends and acquaintances, I don't consciously remember ascribing this unease to my immigrant status. Nor was the unease anything more than an episodic feeling I assumed that everyone experiences at one time or another. But the unease intensified and assumed an ideological dimension during the Vietnam War era. I lost my educational deferment when I left medical school, was called in for a medical examination, and reclassified 1-A for the draft pool. My half-day at the army recruiting center was an eye-opening experience. I confronted American men in whom brutality was officially encouraged in the service of social control and discipline. I wasn't entirely naive, however. I had seen police brutality erupt during several civil rights marches, but we had known that our actions were provocative and part of the strategy was to elicit open hostility in order to expose what we believed was latent state repression. But there was no public good achieved by a bunch of thugs demeaning naked young men during "short-arm" and "cheek-spread" inspections. A rural farm-hand, who was less tractable than most of us "wimpy" college boys, was roughed up a bit just to scare the rest of us. It worked all too well at the moment, but I was so humiliated by this treatment and my own passivity in the face of brutal authorities that I vowed never to place myself in a similar situation again if I could avoid it.

It was 1966, however, and conscientious objection was out of the question on moral grounds without certain religious backgrounds. Moreover, I was politically unsophisticated, knew little about what was going on in Vietnam, and had finished undergraduate school before the war protests filtered into southern campuses. The possibility of going to jail or fleeing the United States simply never occured to me. Foremost in my mind was avoiding the army. Since my draft board gave few educational deferments for graduate school (I had then been accepted for a doctoral program), I knew I needed a back up and applied to the Navy Officer Candidate School. If I had to join the military, maybe I could spend three years vomiting without being yelled at since I would be an officer. I ignored the first letter from the army to report for draft processing, hoping the navy would save me. They did. Soon I would be in training to learn how to defend my country on the high (ugh) seas.

Chance changed my life again, though the miracle I had hoped would keep me out of the navy never occurred. I needed a job for six months until my officer candidate training began, and a school district near the base needed teachers. I was hired to teach twelfth grade civics. I knew enough about the subject to chuck the textbook after two weeks and turn my five classes into history, current events, and problem solving units. Since I would probably be involved in the Southeast Asian theater and most of my students would be confronted with the war in one way or another, I read everything I could find on European and American involvement in the region. At first I refused to believe what I read. I recollect that Bernard Fall gave me many sleepless nights. But I had to teach the material, and I had had enough training in history at that point to allow me to discriminate among the sources. The conclusion was unmistakable. The United States had taken the side of a blatantly authoritarian and ruthless regime, had refused to carry out agreed upon elections because "our guys" would probably have lost, and had turned a civil war in a distant country into a frontal assault against an amorphous Communist conspiracy to destroy "the free world." How could I become part of such a calamitous and destructive charade?

This newfound political disaffection, which I had stumbled upon while trying to enliven boring civics classes, matured into an integrated philosophy of sociopolitical critique of my naturalized homeland during the next decade. My navy experiences were critical to this change and for the parallel and gradual emergence of an expatriate perspective. To mention the highlights of what was a slow, extended process distorts its evolutionary pace, although my experiences do lend themselves to a "punctuated equilibrium" (à la Stephen Jay Gould) interpretation. The first crisis came when I went to talk to a chaplain at Officer Candidate School (OCS) about my discomfort at the likelihood of combatant duty in a war I believed had no morally redeeming purpose whatsoever. I remember contrasting my feelings about Vietnam with the Second World War against fascism, and I even made a point of expressing respect for my father's involvement with the Danish underground. That evening I was unexpectedly ordered to appear before my company officer. He told me that my attitude was unbecoming in a future officer and that he intended to institute proceedings the next morning to have me kicked out of OCS and transferred to the fleet as a seaman recruit. I was frightened and stupefied by this threat. My gut feeling was that he had no right to do it, but this was the United States military where I had few rights. All I could think about was having to spend four years instead of three being bullied in the fleet. Then it dawned on me that the only right I knew I did have had been violated—the chaplain had abused his vow of confidentiality. So I hesitantly asked the basis for the company officer's dissatisfaction with my attitude. When he made some evasive comment about my poor record, I knew I had the advantage, for I had just been appointed cadet company commander for the last month of training—the goal of every sane officer candidate since that rank gave you permission to walk by yourself on the base rather than march in groups and excused you from daily uniform inspections. So I told the company officer that while he could send me to captain's mast, I had the right to call witnesses and intended to call him and the chaplain to explain this sudden change in their evaluation of my performance. He dismissed me, but I heard no more about my attitude until I was in Supply Corps School when the commanding officer there bent over backwards to assign me to a noncombatant ship.

Two years as a supply officer ("Pork Chop" in the navy lingo) brought a different kind of awakening about my lack of harmony with American life—a profound sense of ideological despair. My disaffection with the United States' role in Vietnam and my opposition to combatant duty did set me apart from people in the navy, but these were, by 1967, commonplace responses among people my age, and younger, outside the service. I was on a ship, however, not a college campus, and I had to figure out how to get along with my fellow officers and the rest of the crew. This wasn't difficult to accomplish since I saw no reason to proselytize. All the more astounding and troubling, therefore, was my sense that I didn't really fit in, no matter how much I tried to be one of the guys. At first I attributed this feeling to the fact that I lacked what one might call a military bearing and the military mentality. But this was not a spit-and-polish ship and the officers weren't inflexible martinets. Besides, many of the officers and some of the crew shared my disgruntlement about our involvement in Vietnam. What the officers didn't share was my approach to the enlisted men. They preferred to drink coffee in the wardroom rather than fraternize with the troops in their workspaces, and they insisted on hands-off supervision no matter how much work was left undone when we had skeleton crews aboard. In short, they viewed themselves as "heads," superior to the "hands" who worked, slept, and ate in different places and at a different rhythm. Even more astounding to me, the "hands" accepted this scheme of things as natural to an effective functioning of the system, even though they often grumbled.

Until then, I had always assumed that class distinctions represented a remediable anomaly in American life. It had taken me until my early twenties to realize that class, rather than race, established the great divides in what I had thought, until then, was an egalitarian society. The division I saw between officer and enlisted man in the navy was only a formalization of more complex, but just as palpable, class divisions outside the military. I thought about the divisions among the students I had recently taught in high school: the seniors who expected to work in the costume jewelry factories; the seniors who would get jobs in small businesses, some of which might require vocational training; and the seniors who were in the last year of the college preparatory curriculum. Each group had its own lingo, dress, style, and activity—in short, each group expressed the ethos of their social class. Relatively few expected—or then sought out—opportunities for social mobility, just as the hands and the heads on board my ship largely kept to their places and derided those, like myself, who crossed back and forth as the occasion seemed to warrant. Most of the time I did what I had to do to conform and keep peace. But one evening when I had duty, the thought of sitting alone in the wardroom watching the same film shown on the reel-delay system in the mess hall, whereby one of the deckhands brought me each reel for private showing as they completed it, was more than I could tolerate. Yet the crew felt so inhibited by my presence when I joined them that I left, walked to the fantail, stood for a long time staring at the New York skyline—and realized I was thinking about my my father, my mother, and Denmark.

I recalled having visceral reactions against class bias when I had perceived it in my parents many years earlier and had ascribed it to attitudes from the Old World we had left behind. An aura of class superiority was especially prevalent in my mother in whom I perceived *spidsborgerlig* (philistine) condescension when dealing with shop clerks, our black cleaning woman, tradespeople, and waiters at a segregated country club my father had joined in the late 1950s. My response had been to avoid shopping trips with my mother, to become almost a second son to the cleaning woman, and to sit, whenever possible, with the black workers in their segregated lounge at the country club when I became an employee at the tennis shop. At the time, it was more an act of independence from my Danish parents than a social statement, for I was then unaware that the rest of the membership who knew me disapproved of my behavior more than my parents did. The class biases I perceived in my father seemed more subtle than my mother's, partly because his *borgerlig* (bourgeois) background did not include the pursuit of status so prevalent and intense among the households of minor civil servants at the turn of the century, like the one into which my mother was born. The class biases I associated with my father included his general sense of superiority and the extremely polite, paternalistic dealings he seemed to exhibit with everyone who wasn't a professional. Fair to them or not, that's how I responded to my parents as a teenager. More European elitism and class snobbery, I often said to myself as I swept the tennis courts and strung rackets. All I could think about then was getting away from this tainted heritage as soon as possible. Then it took me another seven years to realize how self-centered and ignorant I had been to miss the fact that the Americans at the country club—members and workers alike—were no less class conscious than my parents, many of them considerably more so. It was startling to realize that evening on the fantail of a "rink" (reserve) destroyer in the old Brooklyn Navy Yard how very little I really knew about the United States, how much less about Denmark. In my attempts to forget the latter and become part of the former, I had distorted both.

Although I date the emergence of my political consciousness to my experiences in teaching high school, my confrontation with the company commander in OCS, and my two years aboard a navy reserve destroyer, I had never really thought about potential cultural

differences associated with my immigrant background until that
evening when I stood on the ship's fantail. I began to wonder whether
the feelings of being different I had often experienced in the past
had had anything to do with being an immigrant in my adopted
homeland. I don't mean the first year or so after coming to the United
States. It was the more recent past that troubled me—all the times
when I had felt like a mutation, as one of my undergraduate profes-
sors once described me. The problem was that I had very little information with which to work. Try as I might on several trips to my
parents' house thereafter, I was unsuccessful in getting them to
open up about what our life had been like in Denmark. Equally
disconcerting was the realization that I couldn't speak or read Danish
any better than the average eight-year-old—in other words, I possessed a child's skills to tackle an adult problem.

By then I was finished with my service obligation and had
just begun graduate school. One thing had become clear to me. My
interest in European history had grown in tandem with the desire to
learn more about my native country. Although I settled on modern
European intellectual history as my general field, I continued to toy
with the notion of doing my dissertation on a Danish topic. At the
time, however, I could only toy with it because I still lacked the
language sophistication to begin serious research. But I was determined to improve those skills. So I said to hell with my embarrass-
ment at reading the books I had saved from my childhood. First I
read my illustrated Hans Christian Andersen, and then I advanced
to Danish translations of Defoe and James Fenimore Cooper—again
in illustrated versions, but the complete editions. After a year of this,
I felt comfortable reading Herman Bang, Martin Andersen Nexø,
Danish history, and Danish newspapers. The latter were especially
disconcerting since I realized I had become more familiar with nine-
teenth-century idioms than the current language. But my scholarly
interests lay in the prior century, anyway, so the handicap seemed
minimal as long as I didn't have to converse with living Danes. After
two years of daily grinding, I had made myself into an anachronism,
more at ease with J. L. Heiberg's popularization of Hegelian philosophy than the columns of *Politiken* that I periodically scanned in
Yale's newspaper room.

When I passed my comprehensive examinations, it was time to sink my lines deeper in Danish waters or cut bait and fish elsewhere for a dissertation topic. I chose to pursue something close to my roots. Twenty years after I had left Denmark, I returned, but by air, landing at Kastrup where I was met by an aunt and an uncle. The automobile trip to Gentofte was like traveling through a time warp. When we arrived at my aunt and uncle's house—maintained much as I remembered it as a child—I felt as if I were eight years old again. Sitting in their garden (it was the middle of May), answering questions about my family and asking about theirs, hidden from the rest of the villa by hedges eight feet tall, speaking Danish with a couple who were a little older than my parents—it was like waking up after a sleep of two decades. Part of my disorientation was attributable to my passage through five time zones and the higher latitude than that to which I was accustomed. But I had the distinct impression that there was something more fundamental at work than jet lag—an impression I had many hours to think about after the sun awoke me at 3:30 in the morning of my first full day in Denmark since 1952.

Later in the morning, my uncle drove me to Copenhagen and dropped me off near Christiansborg Slot since I planned to visit *Det kongelige Bibliotek*. The automobile trip and my unfamiliarity with the library's procedures made me feel like a tourist observing real Danes at work. After slogging through the old catalog system for several hours, I found some promising items, handed in my slips, deposited my notes on a desk, and went for a walk while my requests were processed. I purchased a detailed map of Copenhagen, walked for a bit, found my place, continued walking, got reoriented, walked again, all the while observing what was happening around me. My brief walk became a four-hour exploration of the old city. I finally returned to the garden in front of *Det kongelige Bibliotek*, stood and looked at the goldfish in the pool, and realized that for the first time in twenty years, I felt at home, in myself and in my surroundings. I had never lived in Copenhagen, so the sense of peace and ease was less geographical than ethnic—my sense of identity was with other Danes.

Almost fifteen years have passed since that May afternoon. I have returned to Denmark a half-dozen times since for visits lasting from a few days to several months. Meanwhile, I have settled in Michigan, am happily married, and have a professorial post for the rest of my employable years if I want to keep it. But I still don't feel at home in the United States the way I do in Denmark. My wife and I have often talked about leaving the United States for Denmark or Norway (she's third generation Norwegian, second generation Welsh), but is it fair to do to our children what my parents did to me and my siblings? Moreover, what would we do for a living in Denmark or Norway? We are both teachers, and neither country can employ the teachers generated from within. But even when our children have left home and if we could find jobs in Scandinavia, our parents will be much older and we will not want to be far away from them as they approach their last years. Who knows how old we will be when our parents are dead and our children are on their own? Or maybe we're just afraid to make the change, comfortable enough in everyday life to keep putting off a decision to leave a country in which we feel increasingly uncomfortable for a Scandinavian country that comes closer to our perception of what it means to be part of a community.

    In my mind, the major difference between community values in the United States and Denmark is that whereas Denmark has taken major steps to modify the negative social consequences of the individualistic, liberal, and capitalistic philosophy that we associate with the West, the United States' response has been lackluster and begrudging. Carlyle's condemnation of nineteenth-century England now applies to the United States: the country is rapidly dividing into two camps, the dandies and the drudges. Dandies in the United States are those who draw incomes far in excess of their value to the public good, though many of our dandies grow wealthy because they provide necessary services over which they have unrestricted monopolies. All dandies are social parasites to some degree since they become stockholders who invest their excess earnings with the hope that the underpaid work of the drudges will yield industrial profits so the dandies can, one day, live entirely off their investments. The drudges include the marginally employed, the underemployed, and the unemployed that number in the tens of millions even during the best of times. But if prosperity for the dandies rests on the weakest backs among the drudges of American society, one would think that the country would at least provide the latter with the basic necessities of life. Not so. Reagan's often-touted safety net for the deserving poor has a strange weave to it since each state can make numerous adjustments in the definition of poverty. Therefore, determinations about who should receive benefits, and how much, vary dramatically throughout the United States. It is a scandal that one of the richest nations on earth has millions of people who go hungry (all the time or several days or weeks every month); millions who lack adequate housing, medical and dental care, and livable pensions; and millions who have no job at all or work under debilitating conditions. This scandal is rationalized by the authorities as necessary to preserve the American way of life for everyone.

The frightening thing is that many of the everyones who suffer most from this anachronistic self-help philosophy either accept it as inevitable or defend it because they aspire to join the dandies. Half the voting-age population never bother to register or to cast their ballots in most elections. Civil rights are again under attack as another wave of cold war rhetoric sweeps the country. And decades of inadequate schooling insure that the citizenry are too ignorant and too passive to care about what is going on outside their private lives, to know what their rights are, or to organize collectively to demand change. When groups do organize, it is often for personal material gain—but they are just as often outmaneuvered by the dandies since the self-help philosophy of most contemporary unions is an individualistic philosophy, antithetical to collective activity. In short, most unions in the United States have never developed sociocritical orientations because they espoused the middle-class definition of the American way of life. Only dress and choice of activities separate most American workers from the yuppies (the young urban professionals) who constitute the immediate breeding pool of the privileged dandies in American society. Personal material gain is uppermost in the minds of worker, yuppie, and dandy alike. It occurs to few of them to wonder if their actions serve the public at large, for the public good is an immaterial concept of no relevance to their individual selves.

The eighteenth-century Invisible Hand has reappeared in Reagan's America. Keeping our personal self-interest foremost at all times is the only way to advance the welfare of society at large. The dandies get richer, the drudges get poorer, while the yuppies and the regularly employed working classes provide the buffers between the two classes that hold each other in contempt. Outright rebellion is prevented because both classes and their respective buffer share the same self-help philosophy. But extreme differences in material wealth and opportunities for social mobility have kept American society in the twentieth century as violent as it was in the eighteenth and nineteenth centuries, and such violence continues to rise in tandem with the growth of the self-help philosophy that encourages a focus on the individual and a suspicion of others. Add, as well, the racism, the sexism, the xenophobic ethnocentrism, and the frontier mentality that have deep roots in American history, and one can understand why Americans today live their present lives within a volatile context, considerably more hospitable to rugged individualists than to people concerned about the larger community, particularly those who have difficulty caring for themselves, whether the fault is their own, as one increasingly hears, or whether it lies with the system of which they are a casualty.

Many of the American contributors to this anthology (whether quoted in the introduction or in the complete essays that make up the body of this book) are ill at ease with the inhumane outcomes of the American self-help philosophy in action; but as a group, these Americans seem less clear about the presence of similar attitudes in Danish life, as well as the historical explanation for their presence. Ironically, one major ideological source of the Danish egalitarian and humanitarian perspectives that eventuated in the welfare state has been the United States experiment in democracy. Jacksonian democracy, the Progressive reform era, and the New Deal each served as models for parallel experiments in western Europe—the latter, most forcefully, in Denmark during the 1930s. The question that will probably never be completely answered is why the United States drew back from the creation of a welfare state at the point when

Denmark made its commitment. Undoubtedly, the Resistance experience in Denmark encouraged a break with its past that was without parallel in the United States. Nor can one underestimate the impact of the Danish cooperative movements, the Grundtvigian *højskole* (folk high school) reforms (see chapter 1), and the rise of social democracy in establishing a predisposition for the welfare state—again, without parallels in the United States. Moreover, Denmark had previously exported many of its rugged individualists to America (especially to Utah, Minnesota, and Wisconsin). My parents, for example, are still quite comfortable with the American self-help philosophy that first attracted my father thirty-five years ago. Had they remained in Denmark, it is very probable that my parents would have joined the Glistrupite (Mogens Glistrup is a controversial, post-World War II political figure) reaction against the taxation policies necessary to sustain the welfare state in periods of economic decline.

Glistrup-like individualism was a very powerful force in Denmark until after World War II, so powerful, in fact, that the post war architects of the welfare state avoided a frontal assault on existing economic inequalities. The Danish welfare state that some of the Americans in this anthology consider more humane than the conditions in their native country—as one contributor (Thomas E. Kennedy) writes, "In the States, when you don't have it good, you have it, in my experience, god-awful"—was placed on its present footings by redistributing a substantial portion of the excess profits generated and then heavily taxed during the economic recovery from the 1950s through the mid-1970s. High personal income, corporate and value-added taxes have reduced the most glaring income discrepancies, but class differences continue to exist. Several generations of Danes now accept, by and large, the basic notions of the welfare state and are willing to reduce their disposable income to pay for its continuance. They continue to quibble about the range and degrees of coverage, but there is general agreement on the basic premises. In the wings, however, stand the Glistrupites and other Danes who want to see the government disengage itself from individual lives. A few are remnants of the outmoded landed and industrial aristocracy, but most are the remnants of the laissez-faire individualists whose ranks were depleted by migrations to the United States during the late nineteenth and twentieth centuries. Denmark has fallen on hard economic times again, and the crisis, at the moment, is to convince individual Danes to absorb more and more of the costs of a welfare state until another period of prosperity can lighten the burden again.

Another recurring theme in the anthology is the perception that Danes are much less tolerant of foreigners in the 1980s than they were in the 1960s and early 1970s. One contributor (Ellen Bick Meier) suggests the decade-long economic crisis as a causal factor. I believe she is correct, although one should cast the net a bit wider and examine ethnicity in the context of the economic crisis. Ethnicity is a commonly misunderstood and overused concept. As Peter Worsley has written in *The Three Worlds: Culture and World Development* (London: Wiedenfeld and Nicholson, 1984, 248–249) ethnicity "is always the product of relationships with other economic groups," that is, the outcome of a process of group identification to distinguish itself from others. Danish nationalism is a peculiar form of ethnicity (as is every form of nationalism) that, like others in the West, has evolved through several stages over time. By the middle of the nineteenth century, a hegemonic, chauvinistic nationalism that identified Danishness with a reduced, almost empire-less state defined itself in opposition to the few ethnic minorities, particularly Germans and Norwegians, still included within Denmark's restricted borders. Just as hegemonic nationalism had established itself institutionally, however, another stage of nationalism began to expand by accretion over the hegemonic, like growth rings of a tree. Uniformitarian nationalism reflected the values of the younger middle-classes, especially *studenter*, but also women and the working classes who sought to replace Danish absolutism with liberal, laissez-faire institutional forms that legitimated political participation on the basis of individual rational capacity rather than social or ethnic status. In Worsley's definition, uniformitarian nationalism "is informed by liberal values and assumes that older ethnic identities are now *dépassés*. . . . Since society is the aggregate of its citizens, there are, or should be, no groups, ethnic or otherwise, separating the citizens artifically from the political community as a whole . . ." (252). Danish liberals were successful in this enterprise by the early part of the twentieth century, but they were never able to eliminate the

former—and more "primitive"—hegemonic, ethnic nationalism
that many Danes may dredge up whenever they interact with unwanted foreigners (who often present an equally complex accretion
of nationalisms).

Differing perceptions of ethnicity in changing economic circumstances lie at the core of foreign dissatisfaction with the behavior
of many Danes in the last decade or so. Danes during the postwar
economic boom often welcomed *fremmedarbejderer* (foreign workers) for jobs that Danes wouldn't or couldn't do themselves; Denmark
was, after all, a liberal society where ethnic distinctiveness was
ostensibly secondary, although never quite as theoretically outmoded as in the great, volatile melting pot across the Atlantic. The
Pakistanis and Turks have their own stories about the gaps between
theory and practice in the uniformitarian Danish state, but they
weren't turned back at the border. Note as well how many of the
Americans in this anthology who arrived in Denmark prior to the
mid-1970s found jobs that hastened their process of assimilation into
Danish society. Then, Danes rarely resented the presence of such
foreigners, American or otherwise, as long as there were plenty of
jobs for most and the Danes had their pick of the best. But since
the mid-1970s, the situation has turned nasty. Jobs are fewer and
foreigners are often viewed as ethnically stereotyped competitors
instead of coworkers in a liberal society. Some of the stereotyping
has taken the form of overt racism, although liberal, uniformitarian
legal institutions continue to provide some protection for the increasingly villified ethnic minorities and a basis from which to prose-
cute the Danish racist perpetrators. While one must retain a sense
of proportion—after all, few Danes at present are overt racists and
the overwhelming majority of Danes vehemently condemn racism
and will, I believe, continue to do so—one must also recognize among
Danes a widespread group retreat to the earlier, very familiar, form
of exclusive, hegemonic nationalism that has occurred at the same
time and in constant tension with the de jure liberal nationalism
that defends the civil liberties of foreigners already in Denmark and
refugees seeking entry. The same Danes who pride themselves on
their creation of a welfare state that cares for anyone living in Denmark, regardless of ethnicity, are much less tolerant today of the

foreigners who eat cheese before *sild* (herring) (and, *min gode gud*, on the same plate) or who try to pronounce "the strange glottal noises and indistinguishable gurgles" (as Linda Simonsen characterized them) than they were fifteen years ago. Now such foreigners regularly confront Danes who make impulsive, condescending remarks about uncouth table manners and ridiculous accents. Things have changed in Denmark: it is less hospitable to foreigners than it was in the immediate post war decades, and Danes are more chauvinistic about Danish ways, less tolerant of diversity—in short, ethnically more hegemonic and less liberal than in any previous period in this century.

Americans in Denmark have a particularly difficult time adjusting to this reversion to hegemonic nationalism among Danes because the ideology of liberal, uniformitarian nationalism remains dominant in their native country. Ethnicity for many white Americans, certainly the middle classes, is typically something one observes when "different cultures" put on bazaars in shopping malls on the weekend or when one visits a restaurant in an "ethnic-town" in a big city. Most of the contributors to this anthology appear from the brief biographical sketches to be white, college-educated Americans, albeit considerably more sophisticated about the cultural dimensions of ethnicity than the gawkers I just characterized. Nonetheless, part of the ideological luggage these Americans brought with them to Denmark was the liberal, uniformitarian orientation that ethnicity shouldn't really matter in a welfare state that was also avowedly liberal. But it does matter to Danes. Hegemonic nationalism and an exclusive chauvinistic ethnicity are deeply embedded within the Danish welfare state and will, even in better economic times than now, continue to matter in varying degrees depending on the individual Dane and the economic conditions in that part of Denmark in which Americans find themselves. Note, for example, how frequently the complaint about Danish "coldness and exclusiveness" emanates from Americans who live *i provincerne*, less often touched by the cosmopolitan liberal ethos than in Copenhagen, where most Americans feel relatively comfortable.

There must be another side to the coin, however, that keeps these Americans in Denmark in spite of their dissatisfactions. My reading of the responses to Professor Thomas' questionnaire suggests that many remain, in part, due to their dissatisfactions, because the tensions they experience between old home and new land stimulate their creativity. Limbo is usually uncomfortable for most of us, but it appears to be rich soil for nurturing self-criticism in the contributors to this volume. It also seems to promote the development of what Socrates called the self-examined life that heightens their sensitivities to the new society and cultural values in which they are immersed. The combination of criticism directed inward, including memories of one's past in the United States, and outward at Danish society appears to have generated a self-revitalizing creative momentum among many of the contributors that they understandably wish to retain.

There may be another explanation as well for the conjunction of "limbo" and enhanced creativity evident in this anthology, one that occured to me while reading Oliver Sacks' collection of neurological case studies, *The Man Who Mistook His Wife for a Hat and Other Clinical Tales.* In the introduction, Sacks decries a longstanding bias in neurology for investigating disorders of the left, ostensibly "higher," hemisphere of the brain, the seat of logically specialized and sophisticated functioning. The "primitive" right hemisphere, to the contrary, "controls the crucial powers of recognising reality which every living creature must have in order to survive" (New York: Harper, 1987, 4). The right part of the brain is also the seat of our symbolic, nonverbal, holistic, and synthesizing responses to our surroundings. Sacks' interest in more than just the anatomical-mechanistic ramifications of neurological disorders makes his case studies germane to the situation of immigrant creativity if we accept that the expatriating limbo experience constitutes a psychological disordering in one's familiar and real world. The act of transplacement sets in motion a process whereby the individual seeks "to restore, to replace, to compensate for and to preserve its identity . . ." (6), a process that is highly conducive to creative activity. I noted earlier how the confrontation with customs and a language I didn't understand was like a blow to my left-brain functioning, forcing me to rely upon and develop my right hemispheric activity far more than would have occurred had I remained in Denmark. The outcome of my striving to perserve identity was a new identity—neurologically more integrated but culturally more dissonant than I was before my Atlantic crossing. I am no longer entirely dependent on images, nonverbal sounds, and gestures in order to establish some coherence and happiness in a perplexing world as the neurological disorders in many of Sacks' patients limits them. But struggling with such limits, to whatever degree, in a country where dissonance and unfamiliarity still contribute greatly to my reality, is a major source of whatever creativity I possess. Could I be entirely different from those who crossed the Atlantic in the opposite direction?

For most Americans in this anthology, the American individualistic ethos, although in forms less rugged and blustery than the norm in the United States, has survived immigration to Denmark. These Americans in Denmark will find Danes who share this ethos, but they will never assimilate into Danish society, where community means more than a collection of individuals, unless they question and then de-emphasize their American, extremist individualism accordingly. Danish communal norms have evolved over many centuries, the product of constant adaptation to problems posed by an increasing population within a limited geographical space. As many of the American contributors note, Denmark is a planned society: the countryside is planned, the walking paths are groomed of obstacles, the living rooms are often structured to keep adults contained and children out, visits are approved in advance, dinners are ritualistically organized, and even personal relationships seem to follow some implicit logic of organization and protocol. The contributors to this anthology who view themselves as free-spirited, anything-goes Americans in Denmark may not fully understand how such planning could provide the structure that many Danes consider essential to a fulfilling life. Freedom for Danes is often the security of making personal choices within a relatively, more tightly structured set of collective norms than most adult Americans consider tolerable. Predictable, observed rituals provide the matrix and the routine that many Danes appear to consider essential for their creativity and originality as individuals. The view of individual freedom dominant among the American contributors to this anthology parallels what many northern Europeans term "license": thinking and behavior largely unfettered by communal norms or the personal wishes of other individuals. On the other hand, such relatively (by European standards) unfettered American individualism is often what makes the United States "a culture of allure" (as Kenneth Thomas Tindall put it) to a variety of foreigners, particularly younger foreigners in rebellion against the social norms created by their elders, living and dead. Young Danes are no exception.

But unfettered individualism by Americans in Denmark, even its vestiges among those who try their level best to mute it, often seems brash, gimmicky, even adolescent to many mature and established Danes at ease in *vor lille land.* Such Danes have their own, native, critics. Witness Aksel Sandemose's *Janteloven* (see chapter 1), a caricature of unreflective Danish middle-of-the-roadness that constantly places curbs on overassertive individuals. But whereas most Danes would probably view *Janteloven* (if they have even heard of it) as a useful corrective to the Danish tendency to reproach anyone who doesn't explicitly follow common, agreed-upon rituals and behavioral norms, every American contributor who mentions *Janteloven* does so pejoratively. It represents for these Americans in Denmark a tyranny of the majority at the expense of creative, ambitious individualism; it appears to be "egalitarianism at its worst" (as contributor Bill Heinrich says), leading to ostracism for those who fail to comply; it ostensibly stifles experimentation and new ideas. These American interpretations of *Janteloven* aren't wrong; they reflect a different set of premises about what it means to be a free individual in an open society than the premises shared by most Danes. The outcome of this failure to communicate is detrimental for both ethnic groups, however. It seems to me that Danish society would gain in the long run from the attempt by many well-meaning Americans in Denmark to interject some of the most productive American characteristics—greater toleration of individual diversity, a willingness to take chances more frequently, and infectious intellectual curiosity, among others—into the Danish ethnic identity, broadly construed. In turn, these Americans willing to change their apotheosis of unfettered individualism would gain from a fulsome participation in formulating the welfare state as a viable and humane way of life for everyone in Denmark, indigenous or outsider, for the remainder of this century and part of the next.

What I have just said may strike some Americans in Denmark as incomprehensible or insensitive to their situation as individuals whom Danes will always treat as foreigners. I don't wish to minimize the difficulties of accomodating to a new country that has ethnic identities and cultural values different from one's native land. Nor am I ignorant of the fact that substantial parts of the process of assimilation lie outside the control of the individual immigrant. On the contrary, I am certain that my own immigrant experience, as a Dane in the United States, as traumatic as it has sometimes seemed, doesn't hold a candle to the range of problems faced by the Americans in this anthology who traveled the opposite direction much later in their lives than I did in mine. The age factor is critical. My personality was more malleable, and my capacity to accomodate new values, therefore, much greater than if I had left Denmark for the United States later in life. But if I had an easier time becoming bicultural than most of these Americans suggest they have had, I don't want to minimize the continuing, unresolved problems of my own, incomplete adaptation in the United States. Although few Americans realize that I am Danish without me telling them first, I often feel out of step with the tempo of my neighbors, students, and colleagues. Most of the time I shrug it off as relatively unimportant, although sometimes it troubles me considerably, especially of late. If that trend continues, thoughts about leaving the United States when my parents and parents-in-law are dead and our children established in their own lives will increase as they did during the Vietnam era. If we were to move to Denmark, for example, I know that the discomfort ratio would be inverted rather than eliminated. Like the contributors to this anthology, I too would carry with me strong American attitudes that would cause problems for me among Danes, try as I would to temper them. I too would then have to work as hard as other Americans to shift my self-awareness from a person who left a familiar country, for which they still have many ties, to a person who seeks acceptance in Denmark.

Selected Bibliography

The topic, Americans in Denmark, is virtually unexplored. On the other hand, books on Americans in Europe have been written, but only a few of these deal in any detailed way with the personal problems of immigration or with the relationship of limbo to creativity—two of the central issues of this study. Furthermore, those very few books that focus on Americans who are currently living abroad, deal primarily with Americans who do not intend to stay abroad. Nevertheless, I have included some of the interesting and even marginally relevant books in the field. With the exception of Bainbridge's Another Way of Living: A Gallery of Americans Who Chose to Live in Europe, *studies of immigration to America from Europe (and there are many) more closely parallel this study. I list a few that have been helpful to me, primarily those that I have cited. Annotations accompany some of the following entries.*

BOOKS ABOUT AMERICANS IN EUROPE

Allan, Tony. *Americans in Paris.* Chicago: Contemporary Books, 1977.

Bainbridge, John. *Another Way of Living: A Gallery of Americans Who Chose to Live in Europe.* New York: Holt, Rinehart, and

Winston, 1968. While this book is very different from mine, its conclusions are similar.

Beatty, Jerome. *Americans All Over.* New York: John Day Co., 1940.

Dulles, Foster Rhea. *Americans Abroad.* Ann Arbor: University of Michigan Press, 1964.

Dunbar, Ernest. *The Black Expatriates.* 1968. New York: Pocket Books, 1970. An anthology of interviews, many of which confirm the immigrant's condition of limbo.

Earnest, Ernest. *Expatriates and Patriots: American Artists, Scholars and Writers in Europe.* Durham, N.C.: Duke University Press, 1968.

Hayes, T. L. *American Deserters in Sweden: The Men and Their Challenge.* New York: Association Press, 1971. The men in this study have many of the problems of all immigrants, intensified. Whereas creativity comes to some of them, the struggle to achieve this state of mind is frequently long and arduous.

Lambert, Richard D., ed. *Americans Abroad.* Philadelphia: Annals of the American Academy of Political and Social Science, 1966.

Longstreet, Stephen. *We All Went to Paris: Americans in the City of Light: 1776–1971.* New York: Macmillan, 1972.

McCarthy, Harold T. *The Expatriate Perspective: American Novelists and the Idea of America.* Rutherford, N.J.: Farleigh Dickinson University Press, 1974.

Mowat, Robert Balmain. *Americans in England.* Boston: Houghton Mifflin Co., 1935.

Putnam, Samuel. *Paris Was Our Mistress.* New York: Viking Press, 1947.

Rasponi, Lanfranco. *The International Nomads.* New York: Putnam, 1966.

Ross, Ishbel. *The Expatriates.* New York: Thomas Y. Crowell, 1970.

BOOKS ABOUT AMERICANS IN DENMARK

Hackett, Francis. *I Chose Denmark.* New York: Doubleday, Doran and Co., 1940. Autobiographical account by a writer who left Ireland when he was eighteen, lived in the United States for twenty years, then moved to Denmark with his Danish wife for twenty years before returning to the United States at the outbreak of World War II.

BOOKS ABOUT DANES (AND OTHER IMMIGRANTS) IN AMERICA

Furer, Howard B., ed. *The Scandinavians in America, 986–1970: A Chronology and Fact Book.* Dobis Ferry, N. Y.: Oceana, 1972.

Hale, Frederick, ed. *Danes in North America.* Seattle: University of Washington Press, 1984.

Handlin, Oscar. *The Uprooted.* Boston: Little, Brown and Co., 1951.

Hvidt, Kristian. *Danes Go West.* Skørping, Denmark: Rebild National Park Society, 1976.

Katz, Jane. *Artists in Exile.* New York: Stein and Day, 1983.

Nielsen, George R. *The Danish Americans.* Boston: Twayne, 1981.

Riis, Jacob A. *The Making of An American.* 1901. Reprint. New York: Macmillan Co., 1970. Autobiography of a Dane who immigrated to America.

Scott, Franklin D., ed. *World Migration in Modern Times.* Englewood Cliffs, N.J.: Prentice-Hall, 1968.

Skårdal, Dorothy Burton. *The Divided Heart: Scandinavian Immigrant Experience through Literary Sources.* Lincoln: University of Nebraska Press, 1974.

BOOKS ABOUT DANISH CULTURE

Hansen, Judith Friedman. *We Are A Little Land: Cultural Assumptions in Danish Everyday Life.* New York: Arno, 1980. The author is an American who lived briefly in Denmark.

Thomasson, Ed. *Danish Quality Living.* Copenhagen: Forlaget Folia, 1985. The author is an American immigrant in Denmark.